NATIONAL GEOGRAPHIC
Reach™
Language • Literacy • Content

Program Authors

Nancy Frey

Lada Kratky

Nonie K. Lesaux

Sylvia Linan-Thompson

Deborah J. Short

Jennifer D. Turner

NATIONAL GEOGRAPHIC LEARNING | CENGAGE Learning®

Literature Reviewers

Carmen Agra Deedy, Grace Lin, Jonda C. McNair, Anastasia Suen

Grade 1 Teacher Reviewers

Kristin Blathras
Lead Literacy Teacher
Donald Morrill Elementary School
Chicago, IL

Anna Ciani
ESL Teacher
PS 291X
Bronx, NY

Jonathan Eversoll
*International Baccalaureate
Curriculum Coach*
Park Center Senior High
Brooklyn Park, MN

Barbara A. Genovese-Fraracci
District Program Specialist
Hacienda La Puente Unified School District
Hacienda Heights, CA

Vanessa Gonzalez
ESL Teacher/ESL Specialist
Rhoads Elementary
Katy, TX

Leonila Izaguirre
Bilingual-ESL Director
Pharr – San Juan – Alamo Independent
School District
Pharr, TX

Myra Junyk
Literacy Consultant
Toronto, ON, Canada

Susan Mayberger
*Coordinator of ESL, Migrant and
Refugee Education*
Omaha Public Schools
Omaha, NE

Stephanie Savage Cantu
Bilingual Teacher
Stonewall Jackson Elementary School
Dallas, TX

Annette Torres Elias
Consultant
Plano, TX

Sonia James Upton
ELL Consultant, Title III
Kentucky Department of Education
Frankfort, KY

Acknowledgments
Grateful acknowledgment is given to the authors, artists, photographers, museums, publishers, and agents for permission to reprint copyrighted material. Every effort has been made to secure the appropriate permission. If any omissions have been made or if corrections are required, please contact the Publisher.

Illustrator Credits:
Front Cover: Joel Sotelo

Acknowledgments and credits continue on page 295.

For product information and technology assistance, contact us at
Customer & Sales Support, 888-915-3276

For permission to use material from this text or product, submit all requests online at **www.cengage.com/permissions**
Further permissions questions can be emailed to
permissionrequest@cengage.com

National Geographic Learning | Cengage Learning
1 Lower Ragsdale Drive
Building 1, Suite 200
Monterey, CA 93940

Cengage Learning is a leading provider of customized learning solutions with office locations around the globe, including Singapore, the United Kingdom, Australia, Mexico, Brazil, and Japan. Locate your local office at **www.cengage.com/global**.

Cengage Learning products are represented in Canada by Nelson Education, Ltd.

Visit National Geographic Learning online at **NGL.Cengage.com**
Visit our corporate website at **www.cengage.com**

Printed in the USA.
Quad/Graphics, Versailles, KY

ISBN: 978-13054-02300
ISBN (CA): 978-13054-94541

Printed in the United States of America

17 18 19 20 21 22 23 24

13 12 11 10 9 8 7 6 5 4 3 2

Contents at a Glance

Table of Contents

My Family

? BIG QUESTION

What makes a family?

Read More

 = Comprehension Coach  = Interactive Whiteboard  = NGReach.com

SOCIAL STUDIES

‣ Families
‣ Culture

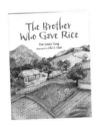

Table of Contents

Shoot for the Sun

? **BIG QUESTION**

When is something alive?

Read More

This Food Grows Here

Seeds

A Bear Eats Fish
David Tunkin

Living Things Need Water

On This Earth

Baby Birds
Neve Koyama

Bricks, Wood, and Stones
Mario Lucca

What Do Pets Need?
Eline Roper

 = Comprehension Coach    = Interactive Whiteboard    = NGReach.com

Unit 2

SCIENCE
▸ Living and Nonliving Things
▸ Plant Parts

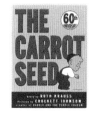

Table of Contents

To Your Front Door

? BIG QUESTION

How do we get what we need?

Read More

 = Comprehension Coach   = Interactive Whiteboard    = NGReach.com

Unit 3

SOCIAL STUDIES
‣ Goods and Services
‣ Needs and Wants

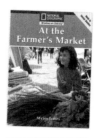
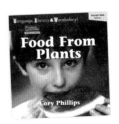

Table of Contents

Growing and Changing

(?) BIG QUESTION

How do animals change as they grow?

Read More

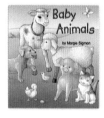

 = Comprehension Coach    = Interactive Whiteboard    = NGReach.com

Unit 4

SOCIAL STUDIES

▸ **Animal Life Cycles**

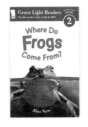

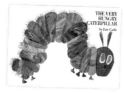

Genres at a Glance

Media

🖥️ = Interactive Whiteboard   🔵 = NGReach.com

My Family

? BIG Question

What makes a family?

Unit at a Glance
▶ **Language:** Describe, Give Information, Social Studies Words
▶ **Literacy:** Plan: Preview, Set a Purpose, and Predict
▶ **Content:** Families

Unit
1

Share What You Know

Do It!

❶ **Draw** your family doing something together. Hang your picture in the classroom.

❷ **Act out** what your picture shows. Can your class find your picture?

❸ **Say** something about your family and the picture.

Build Background: Watch a video about family activities.
NGReach.com

Describe

Listen and sing.   **Song**

Our Routine

My family eats meals.

Dad's lunches are great.

Then I play outside.

I bike or I skate.

When I come home

I help Dad to clean.

Mom reads me a book.

I like our routine!

Tune: "Rock a Bye, Baby"

Key Words

family member

meal

▲ A **family holiday** at **home**.

What is each family member doing? Tell your partner. Name your family members.

Organize Ideas

Idea Web

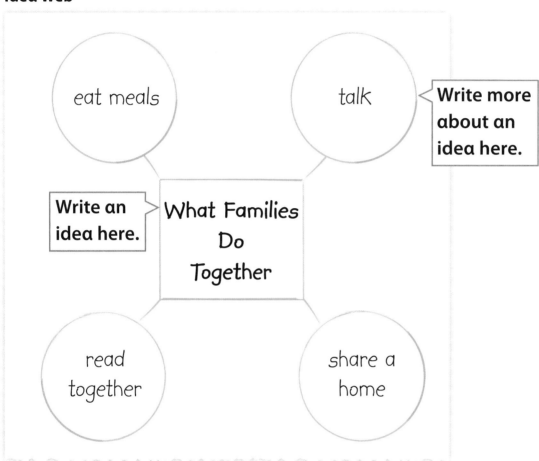

eat meals

talk

Write more about an idea here.

Write an idea here.

What Families Do Together

read together

share a home

Talk Together

Tell your partner what your family does. Make a new idea web. Write in the circles.

More Key Words

care

I **care** for my plant.

celebrate

We **celebrate** grandma's birthday.

• help

I **help** carry the clothes.

play

We **play** a game.

world

There are many people and places in the **world**.

Talk Together

Use one **Key Word** in a sentence.

> I celebrate when I get a good grade.

• High Frequency Word

Add words to My Vocabulary Notebook.
○ NGReach.com

Read a Photo Book

A **photo book** uses photos to tell about real people and things.

✓ Look for **photos**.

Think about what the photos show.

Reading Strategy

Set a purpose before you read. What do you want to learn?

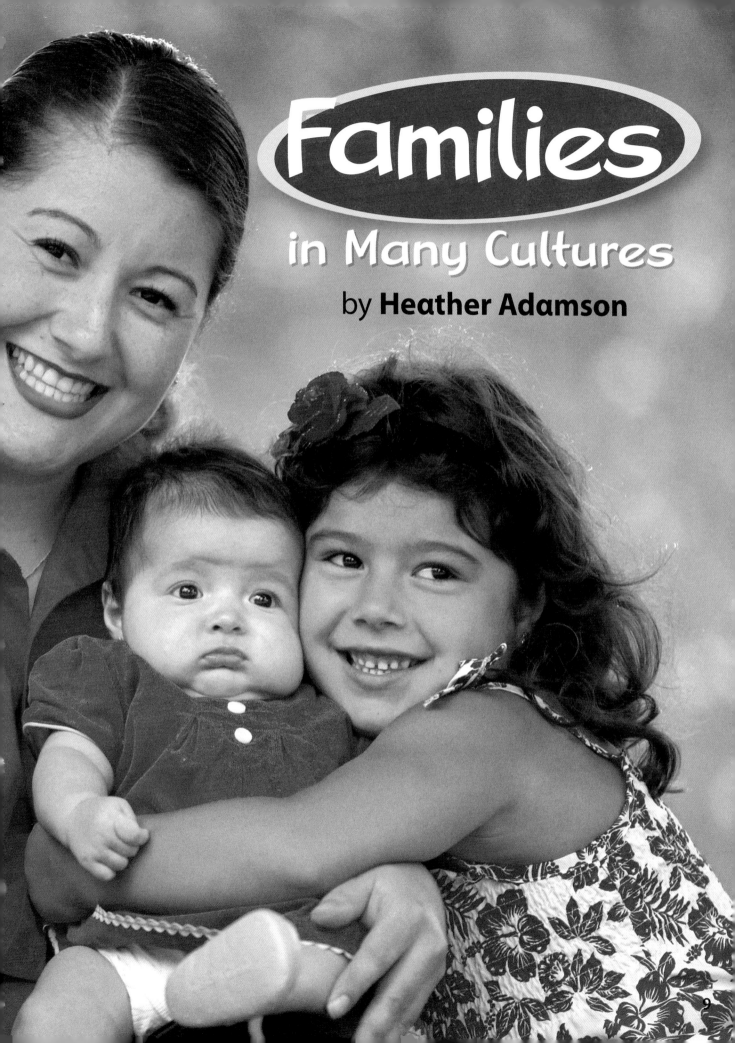

Families

in Many Cultures

by Heather Adamson

Families of all sizes

live around the **world**.

Families help

each other.

Families

share **meals**.

Families **celebrate holidays**.

Families celebrate birthdays.

Families **play** together.

Families laugh together.

What is your family like? ❖

Talk About It

1. What do **families** **celebrate**?

Families celebrate ____ .

2. How are some families the same?

Some families ____ .

3. What purpose did you set for reading?
What did you learn?

I wanted to learn ____ .
I learned ____ .

Learn test-taking strategies.
NGReach.com

Write About It

How does your family **help** you?

My family helps me ____ .

Organize Ideas

What do the families in the story do together?

Idea Web

Use your web. Tell a partner what you learned in "Families in Many Cultures".

The families celebrate birthdays.

Identify Nouns

mother

daughter

daughter

The **mother** has two **daughters**.

A **noun** names a person or people.

Read the list of words. Draw a picture to show each noun. How are the nouns alike?

Nouns
man
baby
sister
teachers

NATIONAL GEOGRAPHIC EXCLUSIVE

Connect Across Texts Learn more about what makes a **family** .

Genre A **magazine article** is nonfiction. It often tells about something going on in the **world** now.

The World Is Your Family

by Josh Thome

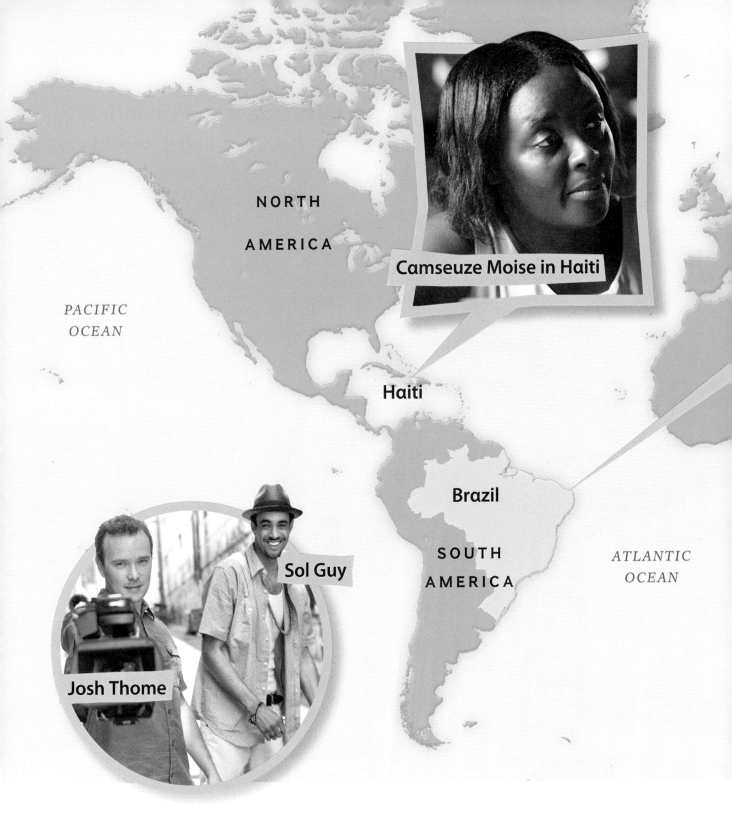

Camseuze Moise in Haiti

NORTH AMERICA

PACIFIC OCEAN

Haiti

Brazil

SOUTH AMERICA

ATLANTIC OCEAN

Sol Guy

Josh Thome

We meet people all over the world.

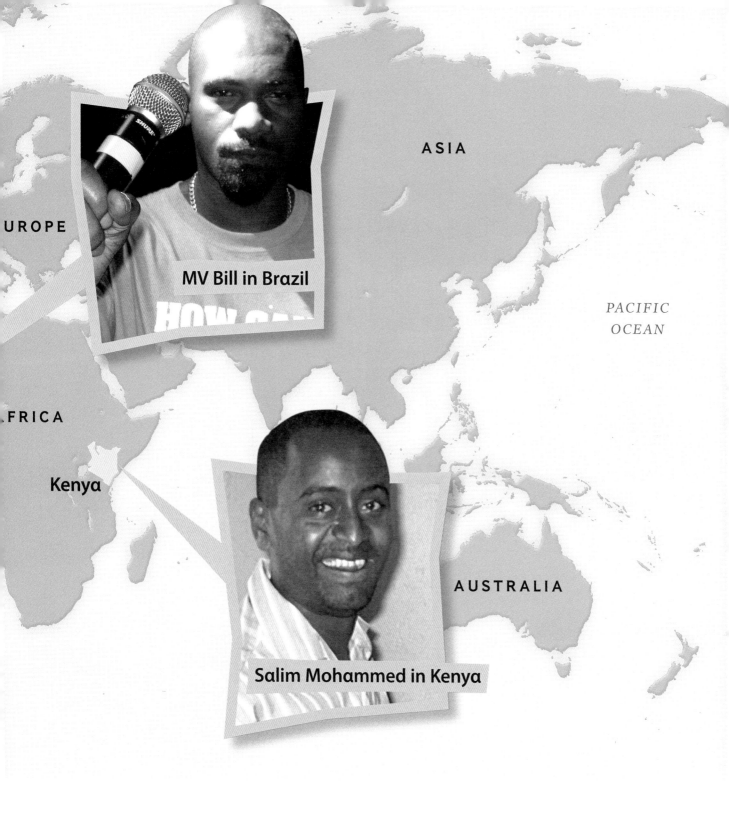

ASIA

EUROPE

PACIFIC
OCEAN

MV Bill in Brazil

AFRICA

Kenya

Salim Mohammed in Kenya

AUSTRALIA

These people **help** others.

Salim Mohammed has a sports program to help kids.

Camseuze Moise teaches about health all over Haiti.

Their message is important.

Singer MV Bill built a community center.

Be family to the world around you.

Compare Author's Purpose

Authors have different purposes for writing.

"Families in Many Cultures"

Families **celebrate holidays**.

16

to share information

"The World Is Your Family"

Singer MV Bill built a community center.

Be family to the world around you.

29

to tell you what they think

Tell another purpose the authors had for writing their texts.

Talk Together

Think about what you read and learned.
What makes a family?

Plural Nouns

A **noun** names one person, place, or thing.

box   home

A **plural noun** names more than one.

boxes   homes

Grammar Rules Plural Nouns

Add **s** to most nouns to show more than one.	Add **es** to nouns that end in **ss**, **x**, **ch**, and **sh** to show more than one.

Read a Sentence

Why do the nouns have **s** or **es**?

We had **sandwiches** for our **meals**.

Write a Sentence

Write a sentence to tell about one of your family's meals. Use a plural noun. Read it to a partner.

Give Information

Listen and sing.   *Song*

Busy Day

I go to Dawes Pool.

This is where I play.

I am with my family.

I have fun today.

I go to Oz Park.

This is where I cheer.

I am with my family.

All the fans are here.

Tune: "Row, Row, Row Your Boat"

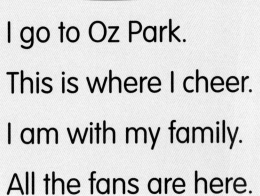

Key Words

Family Photos

This was a **special** day. My **parents** and I saw a parade **together**. It was **fun**!

This is my **extended family**. We **visit** them every year. That is fun, too!

Talk Together

Look at the family photo book. Where do they go? Where do you go with your family?

Identify Setting

Setting Chart

Movie Theater	Picture of the Place
• dark • big • many seats	

Write about a place here.

Draw the place here.

Talk Together

Make a setting chart about a family story you know. Share it with your partner.

More Key Words

group

A **group** has more than two items.

idea

Lori's **idea** is to go to the zoo.

place

The school is a big **place**.

share

We **share** popcorn.

trip

We take a **trip** in our car.

Talk Together

Count the syllables in **Key Words**.

Group has one syllable. Idea has three.

Add words to My Vocabulary Notebook.
○ NGReach.com

Read a Story

Where does this story happen?

At the park, I splash in puddles.

in a neighborhood

Reading Strategy

Preview the story and then **predict**.
What will the boy and Papá do?

Papá and Me

by Arthur Dorros

Good morning, Papá!

It will be a **fun** day.

We cook something new.

We walk. We hold hands.

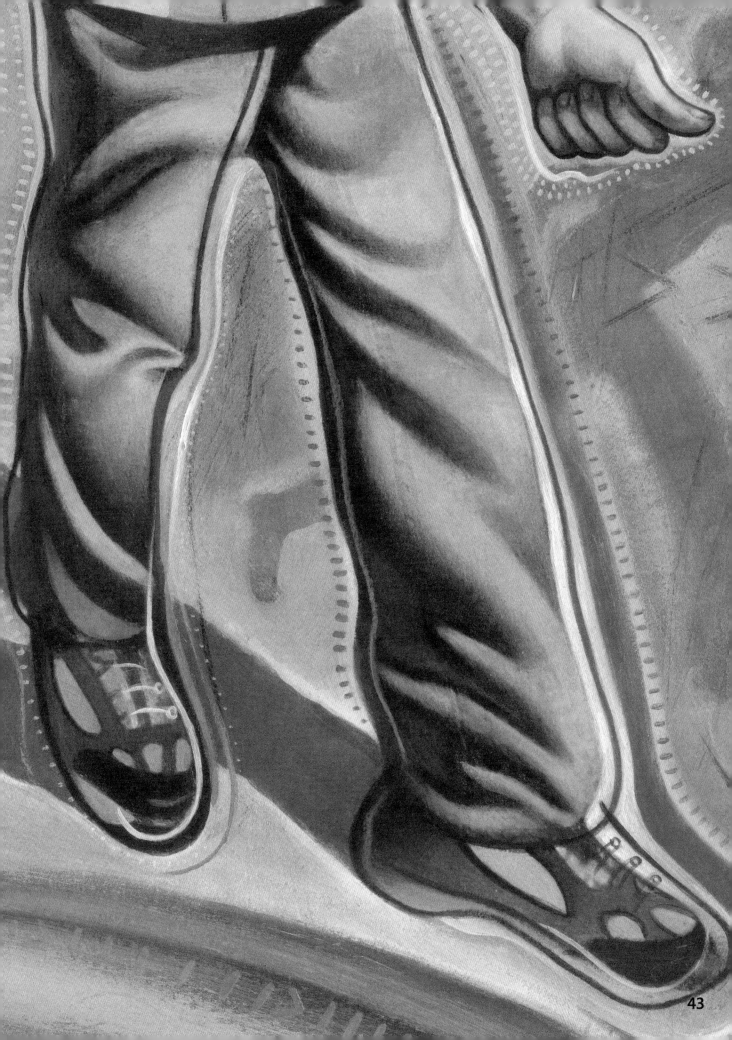

43

At the park, I splash in puddles.

Papá lifts me.

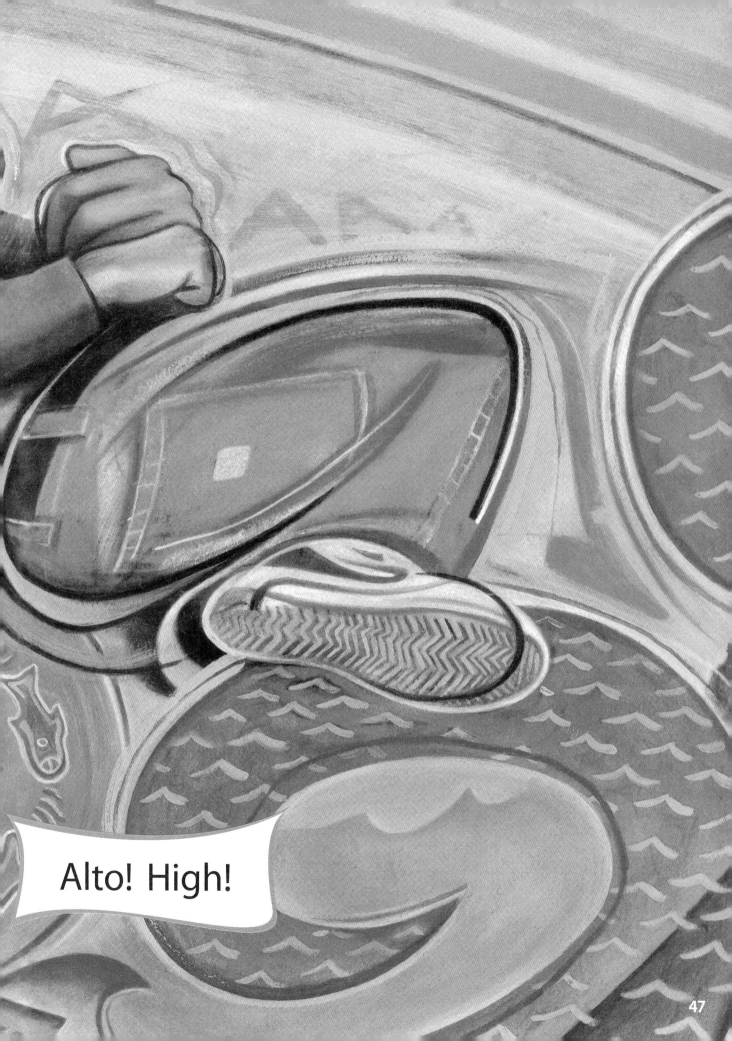

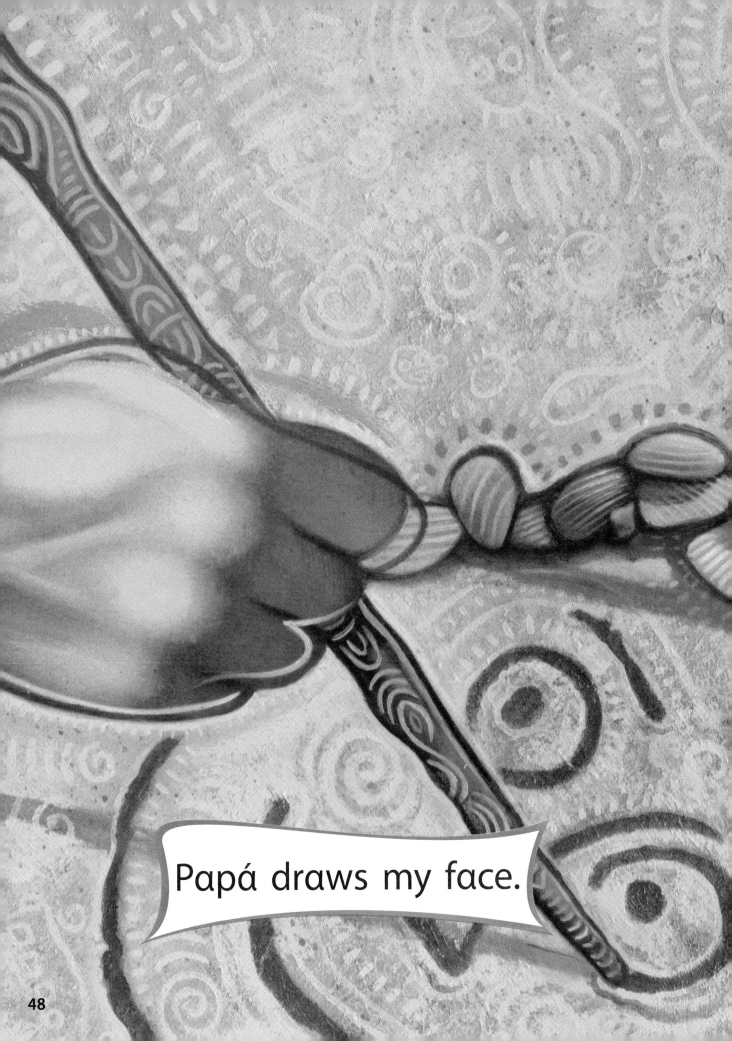

Papá draws my face.

I draw his face.

We **share** stories on the bus.

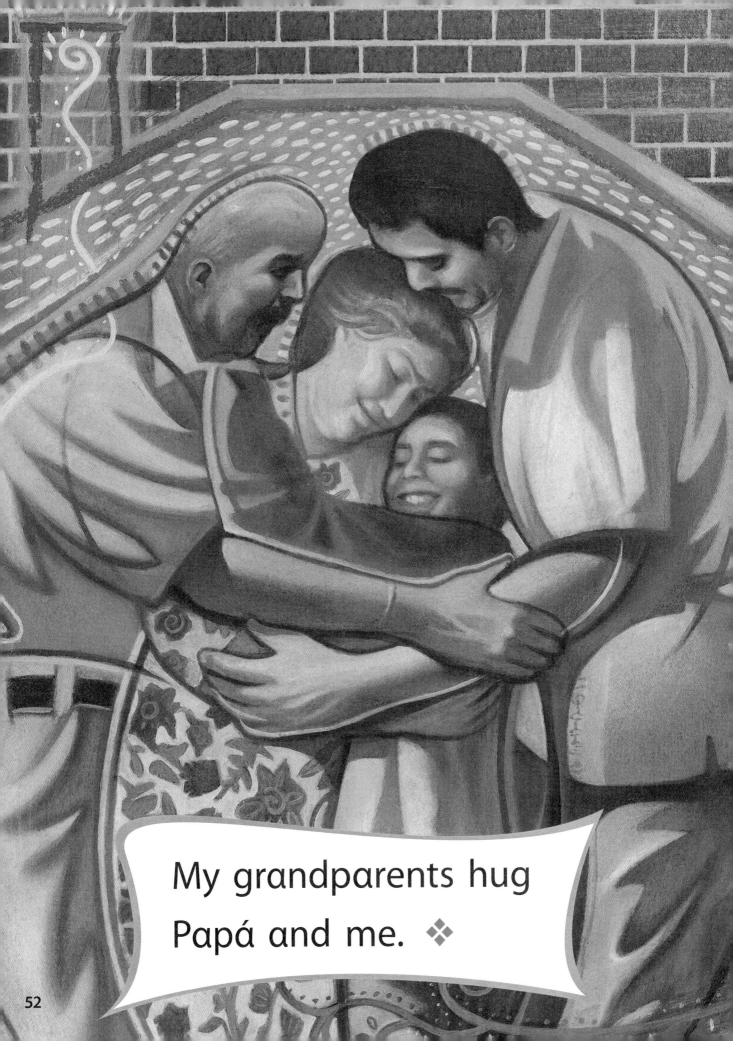

My grandparents hug
Papá and me. ❖

Meet the Author
Arthur Dorros

Arthur Dorros loved to read books when he was a boy. Now he loves to write books!

Mr. Dorros thinks he is very lucky. He grew up with a great dad. Now he has a great son. That is why he wrote *Papá and Me*.

▲ Arthur Dorros

Writer's Craft

In *Papá and Me*, the author shares details about the characters' day together. Write a sentence about one of the characters.

Talk About It

1. What do you see in the pictures of the park?

I see ____ .

2. How can you tell they love each other?

They ____ and ____ .

3. What did you predict they would do? Did your prediction happen?

I predicted they would ____ .
My prediction ____ .

Learn test-taking strategies.
NGReach.com

Write About It

How do you have **fun** with your family?

We like to ____ together.

Identify Setting

Where do Papá and his son go? What are the **places** like? Write words or draw.

Setting Chart

Places	What the Places are Like
• home	• fun
•	•
•	•

Use your chart. Give information about the places in *Papá and Me.*

They go to the park.

Identify Nouns

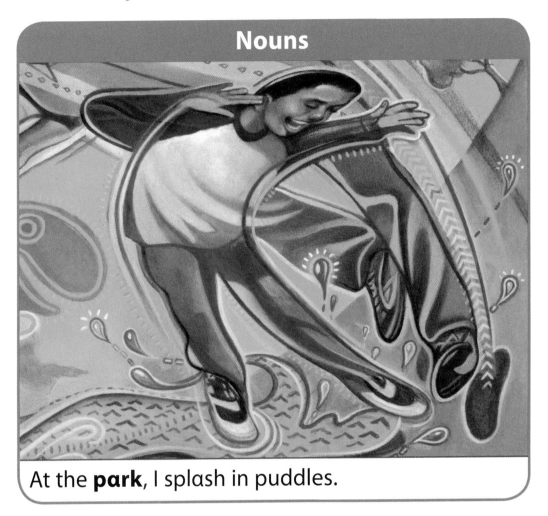

Nouns

At the **park**, I splash in puddles.

A **noun** names a place.

Read the list of words. Which ones are nouns? How do you know?

| go |
| home |
| library |
| play |

Connect Across Texts Read more about what makes a family **special**.

Genre A **postcard** is like a letter. You send it in the mail.

Postcard to Grandpa

by **Amy Tong**

Greetings from ARIZONA

March 15

Dear Grandpa,

Arizona is so **fun**. I like riding the horses. You should come to this **place**.

We miss you!

Love,

Amy

To: Grandpa Tong

820 Sunnybrook

Greenhill, Wisconsin 93759

Compare Genres

How are *Papá and Me* and "Postcard to Grandparents" different?

Realistic Fiction

We **share** stories on the bus.

The story is made up, but it seems real.

Postcard

March 15

Dear Grandpa,

Arizona is so **fun**. I like riding the horses. You should come to this **place**.

We miss you!

Love,

Amy

The postcard is a message from a real person.

Talk Together

Think about what you read and learned.

What makes a family?

Proper Nouns

A **proper noun** is the name of a special person, animal, or place.

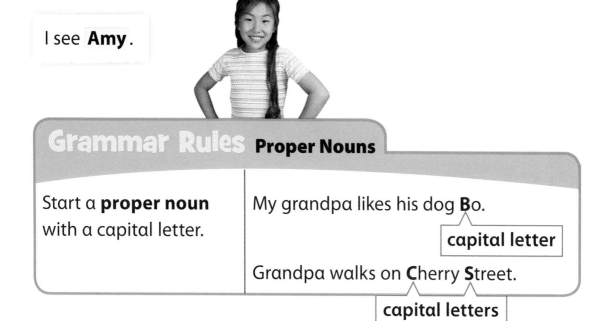

I see **Amy**.

Grammar Rules **Proper Nouns**

| Start a **proper noun** with a capital letter. | My grandpa likes his dog **B**o.
 capital letter
 Grandpa walks on **C**herry **S**treet.
 capital letters |

Read a Sentence

Why does Chávez Park have capital letters?

Papá and I went to Chávez Park.

Write Sentences

Write a sentence about a family member. Use the name of your family member in the sentence. Read it to a partner.

61

Write as a Family Member

Write a Photo Essay ✏️

Where does your family go? Tell about a special place. Write a photo essay for your family.

Our Family Place

by Bali Rashidi

A photo essay has photos.

We go to **Camp Blue Lake**.

Captions give information about the photos, like the **setting** or people pictured.

This is where we cook outside.

❶ Plan and Write

Work with a partner. Talk about places you go with your family. Pick one place. Find photos or make drawings of the place. Tell your partner about the place.

Write about where you go. Then write about why the place is special. Match each sentence with a picture.

❷ Check Your Work

Revise and edit your writing. Use this checklist.

❸ Finish and Share

Finish your photo essay. Write each sentence neatly. Leave space between words.

Read your photo essay aloud. Hold up the photos so that the group can see. Sit quietly while others speak. Share what you know.

Checklist

☑ Think about different nouns you can use. Can you use nouns that name people and places?

☑ Check your sentences. Did you begin names of special places with a capital letter?

☑ Read each line of your work. Keep track of words you misspell. Make your own spelling list.

I have fun with my family!

Share Your Ideas

Think about the things families do together. What makes a family? Choose one of these ways to share your ideas about the **Big Question**.

Write It!

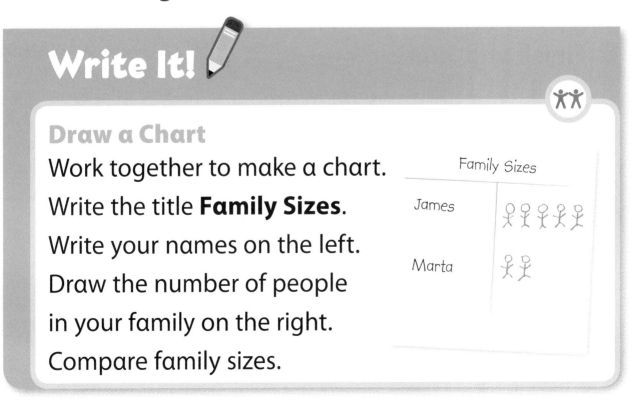

Draw a Chart

Work together to make a chart. Write the title **Family Sizes**. Write your names on the left. Draw the number of people in your family on the right. Compare family sizes.

Family Sizes

James

Marta

Talk About It!

Plan a Family Trip

As a group, plan a great family trip. Make a list of where you would go, what you would do there, and how you would get there. Locate the places on a map.

We would take a train.

Do It!

My Helping Hands

Trace your hands on a piece of paper. Write one way you help out at home on each finger.

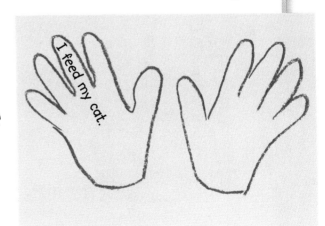

I feed my cat.

Shoot for the Sun

? BIG Question

When is something alive?

Unit at a Glance
▶ **Language:** Describe, Retell a Story, Science Words
▶ **Literacy:** Monitor
▶ **Content:** Living and Nonliving Things

Unit
2

Share What You Know

Do It!

❶ **Think** of something that is alive.

❷ **Act Out** how it moves. Have the class guess what it is.

❸ **Share** your picture. Tell what else the living thing can do.

Build Background: Watch a video about how a plant grows.
◯ **NGReach.com**

Describe

Listen and sing.   **Song** ((MP3))

I Love My Bike

I can eat and I can drink.
I am living.

I am healthy. I can think.
I am a living thing.

My bike can not eat.
My bike can not play.
It's nonliving.
That's OK.
I love it anyway!

Tune: "Camptown Races"

Key Words

People, plants, and animals are **living** .

Talk Together

You are living. How do you know? Describe how something nonliving is different from something living.

List Facts

Living Things Checklist
can eat ☑
can drink ☑
is healthy ☑
can think ☑

List facts about living things here.

Check off the facts here.

Look and listen for facts in texts that you hear and read.

It's nonliving!

Talk Together

Choose a **living** or **nonliving** thing in the classroom. Have a partner guess what it is using the checklist and other questions.

More Key Words

alive

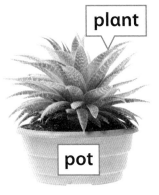

plant

pot

A plant is **alive**.
A pot is not alive.

energy

Swimming takes
a lot of **energy**.

exercise

My heart beats
fast when I
exercise.

food

I like many kinds
of **food**.

health

Brushing your
teeth is good for
your **health**.

Talk Together

Use one **Key Word**
in a sentence.

I have a lot of
energy today.

Add words to My Vocabulary Notebook.
NGReach.com

Read a Song

A **song** is words with music. You can sing a song.

✓ Look for **rhyme**. Listen to the **rhythm**.

Can it fly? Can it run by?

rhyme

Reading Strategy

Monitor your reading. When is something alive?

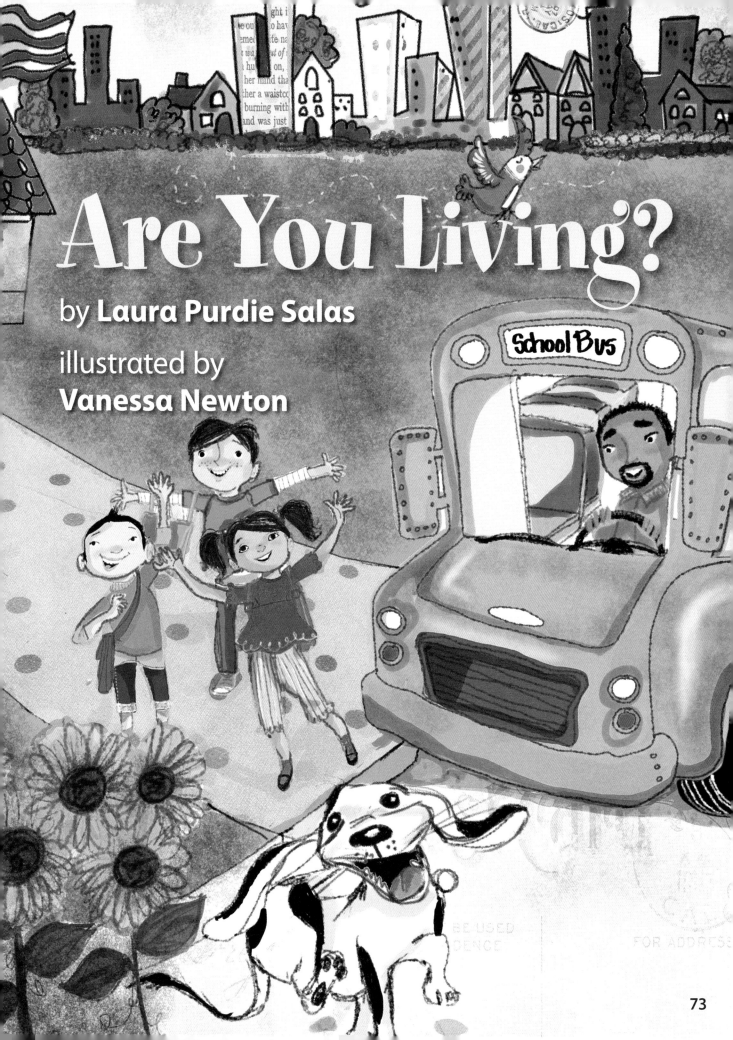

Are You Living?

by **Laura Purdie Salas**

illustrated by
Vanessa Newton

Are you **living**? Are you living?

Do you **eat**? Do you sleep?

If you need to **breathe** air,
Move from here to there, then

You're living. You're living.

Is it growing? Is it growing?

Toward the sky? Green and high?

If it needs damp ground and
Sunshine all around, then

It's a plant. It's a plant.

Is it moving? Is it moving?

Can it fly? Can it run by?

Living things need dinner,
Or they get much thinner.

So they need
To **drink** and feed. ❖

Talk About It

1. What happens to a **living** thing if it does not **eat**?

   If a living thing does not eat, it will ____ .

2. What helps a plant grow tall?

   ____ helps plants grow tall.

3. How do you know if something is **living**?

   Something is living if ____ .

Learn test-taking strategies.
⬤ NGReach.com

Write About It

Living things **move** in different ways.
How do you like to move?

I like to ____ and ____ .

List Facts

What other facts did you learn about living things? Add to the checklist.

Living Things Checklist

can eat	✔
can drink	✔
is healthy	✔
can think	✔
	☐
	☐
	☐

With a partner, look through the pictures in the song. What is living and nonliving in each picture? Use your checklist.

The flower grows.

I grow, too.

Sort Words

Living Things	Nonliving Things
boy	ball
dog	flag
plant	clock

You can sort these words in a group because they are alike. They are all **Living Things**.

You can sort these words in a group because they are alike. They are all **Nonliving Things**.

Try It Together

Use picture cards. Sort the words into two groups. Talk about how the words in each group are alike and different.

Connect Across Texts You read about what makes something **living**. Now read about how one living thing becomes **nonliving**.

Genre A **diagram** uses steps to show how something is made.

A Straw Hat

by **Lily Block**

1 These living plants grow tall and green.

2 A farmer cuts down the plants. The farmer collects the plants.

Straw begins as a **living** thing.

3 The dry plants are straw.

4 The straw is made into a hat. The hat is nonliving.

A straw hat is a **nonliving** thing.

Compare Genres

How are "Are You Living?" and "A Straw Hat" different?

Song

Toward the sky? Green and high?

rhyming words

79

Diagram

1 These living plants grow tall and green.

2 A farmer cuts down the plants. The farmer collects the plants.

Straw begins as a **living** thing.

90

numbered steps

Talk Together

Think about what you read. When is something **alive**?

Grammar

Skills Trace: ▶ Adjectives: Color, Size, and Shape 🔄 ○
▶ Adjectives: How Many/How Much 🔄 ○
⊙ **Adjectives:** Color, Size, and Shape

Adjectives

An **adjective** describes, or tells about, a **noun**.

A **red machine** collects the **tall plants**.

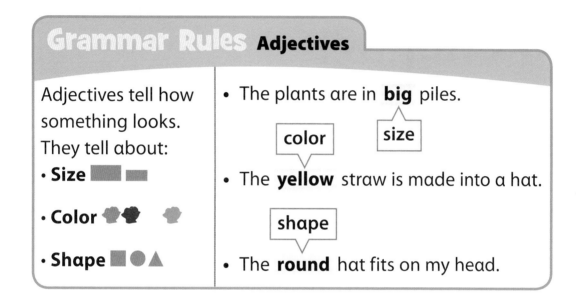

Grammar Rules Adjectives

Adjectives tell how something looks. They tell about:	• The plants are in **big** piles.
• **Size** ▬▬ ▬	color size
• **Color** ❀❀ ❀	• The **yellow** straw is made into a hat.
• **Shape** ■●▲	shape
	• The **round** hat fits on my head.

Read a Sentence

Which words below are adjectives? How do you know?

The red ribbon is on the small hat.

Write a Sentence

Think about a shirt you have. Write a sentence to tell about it. Use an adjective. Read the sentence to a partner.

93

High Frequency **Words**
had
that
will

Retell a Story

Listen and sing. *Song* ((MP3))

Ant and the Grasshopper

I **will** retell a story
About a smart ant
And a lazy grasshopper
That did not like to plan.

In the hot summer,
Ant looked for seeds.
When winter days came,
Ant **had** good food to eat.

Grasshopper did not work.
All summer he played.
But then he was hungry
On cold winter days.

Tune: "On Top of Old Smokey"

94

Key Words

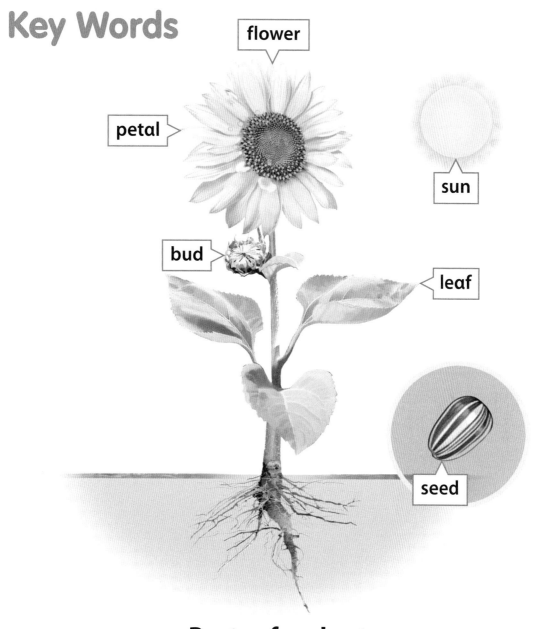

flower

petal

sun

bud

leaf

seed

Parts of a plant

Talk Together

Look at this living plant. Talk about its parts.
Use the diagram to make up a story. Retell the
story to a friend.

Identify Plot

Character-Setting-Plot Chart

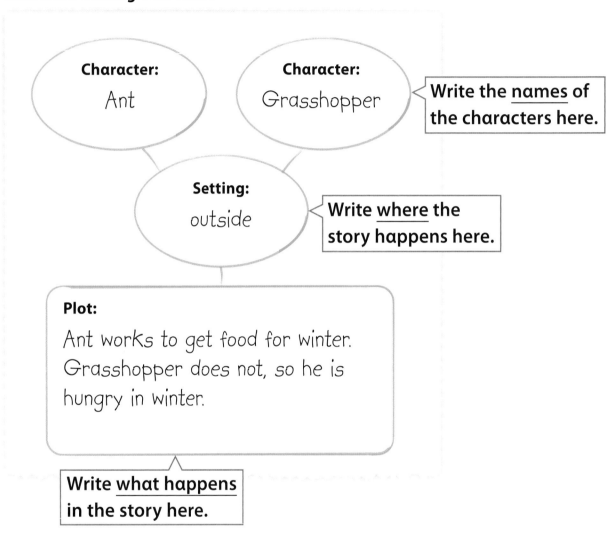

Character:
Ant

Character:
Grasshopper

Write the **names** of the characters here.

Setting:
outside

Write **where** the story happens here.

Plot:

Ant works to get food for winter. Grasshopper does not, so he is hungry in winter.

Write **what happens** in the story here.

Talk Together

Retell a story you know to a partner. Write the title. Then fill out a character-setting-plot chart. Take turns.

Academic Vocabulary

height

This basketball player's **height** is seven feet.

length

The **length** of the carrot is 7 inches.

light

The **light** is bright.

project

I am so proud of my science fair **project**.

ready

The runner is **ready** to race.

Talk Together

Ask a question using a **Key Word**.

What is the height of that tree?

Add words to My Vocabulary Notebook.
○ NGReach.com

Read a Folk Tale

What happens in the folk tale?

A folk tale has a **plot**. A plot is what happens in a story.

A seed sleeps.

The seed becomes a flower.

Reading Strategy

Monitor your reading. What happens to the seed?

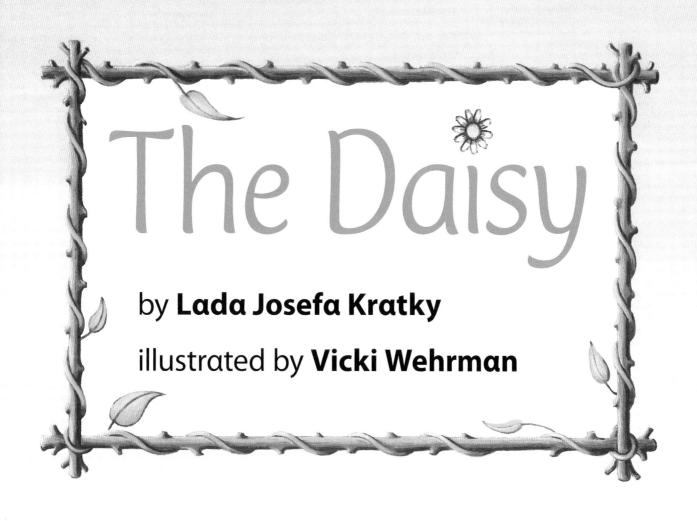

The Daisy

by **Lada Josefa Kratky**

illustrated by **Vicki Wehrman**

A little **seed** sleeps under the earth.

The **sun** shines. The rain falls.

One morning, the sun rises.

The sun knocks on the door.

The sun asks the little seed to come out and play.

The little seed says she just wants
to sleep.

A raindrop knocks on the door.

The raindrop asks the little seed to come out and play.

The little seed says she just wants
to sleep.

The little seed goes back to sleep.

Time passes. The sun rises.
More rain falls.

The sun and the rain knock on the
little seed's door.

The door opens. A **leaf** grows. Then
a little **bud** grows.

One **petal** opens. Then many
more open!

The little daisy smiles.

The daisy says hello to her friends.

She is **ready** to play now.

The sun, the rain, and
the daisy play together. ❖

Meet the Author

Lada Josefa Kratky

Lada Josefa Kratky grew up in Uruguay. Today she lives in California.

Lada writes books in both English and Spanish. She has written many wonderful folk tales!

▲ Lada Josefa Kratky

Writer's Craft

Find details that Lada Josefa Kratky uses to describe how a seed grows into a flower. How do the details help you understand what happens?

Talk About It

1. What does the little **seed** grow up to be?

The little seed grows up to be a ＿＿ .

2. Why do the **sun** and the raindrop knock at the little seed's door?

They want the little seed to ＿＿ .

3. How do the sun and the raindrop help the little seed?

They give her ＿＿ .

Learn test-taking strategies.
NGReach.com

Write About It

What does a seed need in order to grow?
Write one sentence. Read it aloud.

A seed needs the sun to grow.

Identify Plot

Complete the chart for *The Daisy*.

Character-Setting-Plot Chart

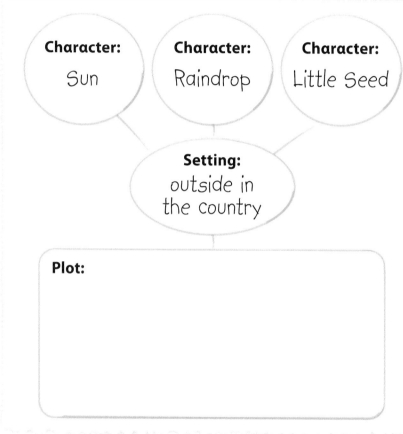

Character: Sun

Character: Raindrop

Character: Little Seed

Setting: outside in the country

Plot:

Use your character-setting-plot chart to describe what happens to the little seed.

The little seed will not play with the sun because she only wants to sleep.

Sort Words

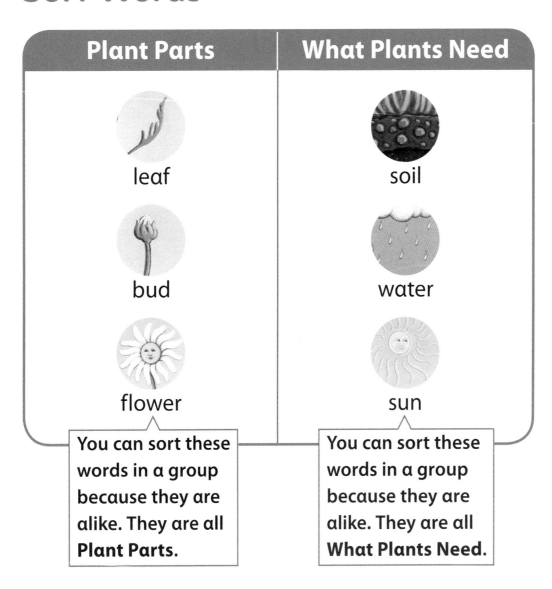

Plant Parts	What Plants Need
leaf	soil
bud	water
flower	sun

You can sort these words in a group because they are alike. They are all **Plant Parts**.

You can sort these words in a group because they are alike. They are all **What Plants Need**.

Try It Together

Write the words on cards. Sort the cards into two groups: **Kinds of Plants** and **Where Plants Grow**. Talk about why each word belongs in its group.

daisy
garden
flowerpot
sunflower

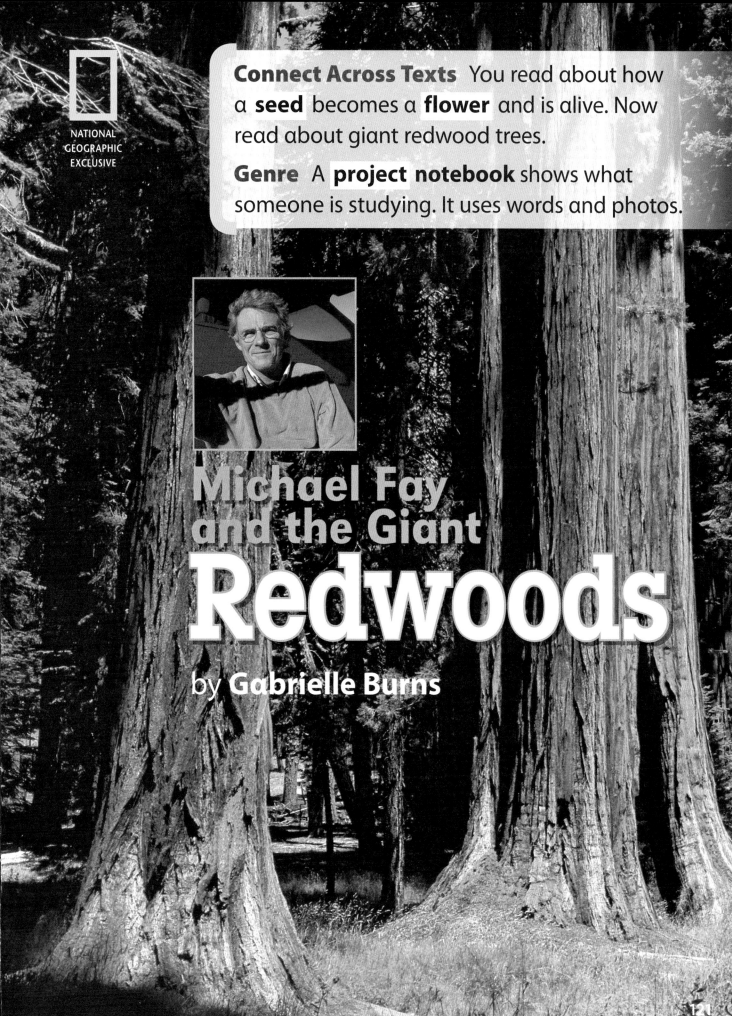

Connect Across Texts You read about how a **seed** becomes a **flower** and is alive. Now read about giant redwood trees.

Genre A **project notebook** shows what someone is studying. It uses words and photos.

NATIONAL
GEOGRAPHIC
EXCLUSIVE

Michael Fay and the Giant
Redwoods

by **Gabrielle Burns**

Michael Fay studies redwood trees.
They are one of the biggest living
things on Earth!

Redwood trees can grow to a **height** of 360 feet!

Redwood Coast

CALIFORNIA

Redwoods grow in California.
California has what redwoods
need to grow.

Redwoods need warm, wet weather. They get a lot of water from fog.

Compare Genres

How are the words in *The Daisy* and "Michael Fay and the Giant Redwoods" different?

Folk Tale

The little seed says she just wants to sleep.

108

A folk tale is a fantasy.
A seed can talk.

Project Notebook

Redwood trees can grow to a **height** of 360 feet!

123

A project notebook is nonfiction. It has facts.

Talk Together

Think about what you read. When is something alive?

Adjectives

An **adjective** describes, or tells about, a **noun**.

One child sees many trees in the forest.

Grammar Rules Adjectives

Adjectives tell **how many** or **how much**.	• Michael walks **two** miles.

how many

• He stands next to **several** trees.

how much

Read a Sentence

Which word below is an adjective? How do you know?

Michael photographs five trees.

Write a Sentence

Write a sentence that describes the redwoods. Use an adjective that tells "how many" or "how much".

Write Like a Teacher

Write How to Make Something

You can make a hat with straw.
What else can you make with plants?
Explain how to make something with
plants. Write for your classmates.

How to Make a Seed Picture

by Pham Thi Mai

What You Need

list > pencil   paper
glue   seeds

What You Do

directions > 1. Draw a picture on the paper.

2. Put glue on the parts of
the picture where you
want seeds.

3. Press the seeds onto the glue
Let it dry.

- I need ____.
- The steps are ____.

❶ Plan and Write

Talk with a partner about plants and plant parts. Draw pictures of what you can make with plants. Pick one thing and describe it to your partner.

Write what you will need. Then write what to do. List the steps in order.

❷ Check Your Work

Revise and edit your writing. Use this checklist.

❸ Finish and Share

Finish your writing. Leave space between steps. Number the steps. Draw a picture to show each step.

Read your writing aloud. Speak clearly. Share what you know.

Checklist

☑ Think about the group, What You Need. Did you remember to write all the things that belong in this group?

☑ Did you use adjectives to describe how things look or feel?

☑ Read each word of your work. Say aloud the syllables. Circle words to check. Correct spelling errors.

I need sunflower seeds.

Share Your Ideas

Think about what living things do and what they need. When is something alive? Choose one of these ways to share your ideas about the **Big Question**.

Write It!

Make a Chart

Draw a T chart. Write these headings: Living Things and Nonliving Things. Draw and label pictures to go under each heading.

Talk About It!

Tell a Tale

Make up a new folk tale about a plant and a rock. The group decides on character names and a setting. Then, each person in the group tells part of the plot. Take turns.

> A small plant and a big rock lived in the forest.

Do It!

Make a Puppet

Use a sock to make a puppet of Zina. Then make Zina come alive! Show what she can say and do. Use your sock puppets to have a puppet show.

To Your Front Door

BIG Question

How do we get what we need?

Share What You Know

❶ Draw a picture of a fruit that you like.

Do It!

❷ Tell where you think it was made. How do you think it got to you?

Build Background: Watch a video about markets.
◯ NGReach.com

Express Needs and Wants

Listen and sing.   **Song**

To Market

I **need** peas.

I need fish.

These two **things**

Are on my list.

At the market

They sell toys

Both big and small.

I **want** a car.

I want a ball.

Tune: "This Old Man"

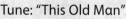

134

Key Words

At the **market**

▲ They **shop** at the market. They **buy** food.

Talk Together

Look at the market. What do you need to buy at the market? What do you want to buy?

Categorize

T Chart

Need	Want
• peas	• toy car
• fish	• ball
•	•
•	•

On one side of the chart, list what you need.

On the other side, list what you want.

Talk Together

Choose eight picture cards. With a partner, sort them into Wants and Needs piles. Then add the items to the chart.

More Key Words

business

My father owns a flower **business**.

• goods

Stores sell these **goods**.

job

My mom has a **job** at a bank.

• needs

Food and clothing are **needs**.

• wants

Toys and games are **wants**.

Talk Together

Give clues for a **Key Word** for a partner to guess.

This word can be a store. It starts with a b.

• High Frequency Word

Add words to My Vocabulary Notebook.
○ NGReach.com

Read a Social Studies Article

A **social studies article** is nonfiction.
It tells about real things.

✓ Look for headings.

Markets sell fish.

Reading Strategy

Ask questions as you read. What kinds of markets are there?

Markets

by Cassie Mayer

Markets Around the World

People **shop** at **markets**.

Markets **sell** many things.

spices

People sell things at markets.

People **buy** things with **money**.

Types of Markets

Markets are big.

Markets are small.

Markets are on streets.

Markets are in malls.

What Markets Sell

Markets sell fish.

Markets sell cheese.

Markets sell clothes.

Markets sell toys.

Markets are special wherever
you go.

People **need** markets. ❖

Talk About It

1. Name three things that **markets sell**.

Markets sell ____ , ____ , and ____ .

2. How are markets different?

Some markets ____ . Some markets ____ .

3. Why do people **need** markets?

People need markets to ____ .

Learn test-taking strategies.
NGReach.com

Write About It

Write two questions you had as you read about markets.

What is ____ ?
Where ____ ?

Categorize

Markets are alike and different. What do they sell?

T Chart

Type of Market	What it Sells
• fruit market	• bananas, pears, grapes
•	•
•	•

Use your chart. Tell a partner what you learned in *Markets*.

> Markets sell fish and cheese.

Identify Verbs

Buy and **sell** are **action verbs**. An action verb tells what someone or something does.

> She **buys** lettuce.
> He **sells** vegetables.

Try It Together

Talk about these words. Act out the words that are action verbs.

desk	man
shop	clap
jump	orange

NATIONAL GEOGRAPHIC EXCLUSIVE

Connect Across Texts Read more about how **goods** are sold to get people what they **need** and **want** .

Genre An **online article** is a story or text on the Internet.

Flower Power

by Stefanie Boron

Farmers Sell Flowers to Save Land

by **Stefanie Boron**

September 21, 2009– Farmers in Brazil grow crops. Cid Simoes and Paola Segura had an idea to help farmers save land.

▲ **Cid Simoes and Paola Segura**

▲ These are soybean crops. They need a lot of land to grow.

NEXT »

The forests of Brazil have beautiful plants and flowers. People around the world want to **buy** them.

Farmers can **sell** these plants and flowers instead of crops.

▲ Brazilian orchid

▲ Orchid **market**

« PREVIOUS

Compare Author's Purpose

Articles have different topics. Authors write articles for different reasons.

Markets

People **shop** at **markets**.

140

The topic of this article is markets around the world.

Flower Power

The author's purpose for writing this article is to tell about flower farmers in Brazil.

Talk Together

Think about what you read and learned. How do we get what we need and **want**?

Present Tense Verbs

Some **verbs** tell about actions that happen **in the present**. The actions happen **now**.

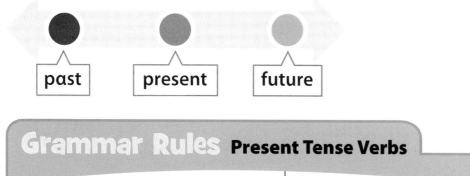

| past | present | future |

Grammar Rules Present Tense Verbs	
Tell what one person or thing does now.	Use **s** at the end of the verb.

Read a Sentence

Why does the verb below have **s**?

The girl **buys** flowers.

Write a Sentence

Write a sentence about a farmer in Brazil. Write about what a farmer does now. Read it to a partner.

Ask Questions

Listen and sing. **Song**

Shopping

I want to buy this set of markers.

Where can I buy all of them?

What other things can I get there?

I also need red and blue pens.

Let's go, let's go.

Let's go today to the

office store.

Let's go, let's go.

How do we get to the store?

Tune: "My Bonnie Lies Over the Ocean"

Key Words

Shoes to You: A How-to

1. Make it in a **factory**.
2. Send, or **ship**, it on a truck.
3. The **delivery** comes to the **store**. Buy it!
4. Bring it home to your **neighborhood**.

Talk Together

Use the picture. Follow the steps in order. Ask a partner questions about how shoes get to your neighborhood.

Identify Details

Idea Web

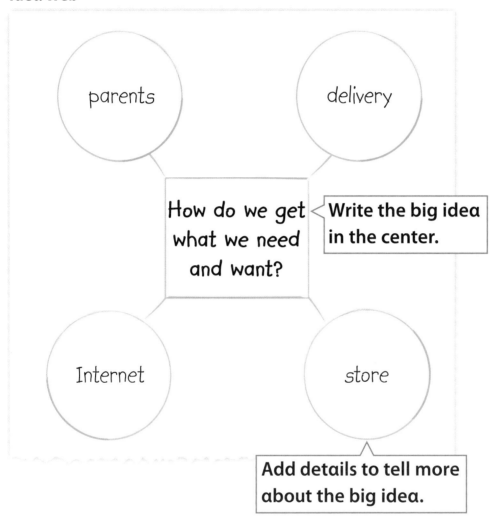

How do we get what we need and want?

parents

delivery

Internet

store

> Write the big idea in the center.

> Add details to tell more about the big idea.

Talk Together

Make an idea web. Write "What do I need for school?" in the center. Fill in the details. Share it with a partner. How are your details the same?

More Key Words

bring

I **bring** my backpack to school.

count

I **count** my money to see what I can buy.

earn

The boy works to **earn** money.

service

A **service** is work someone does for money, such as cutting hair.

worker

A **worker** at the restaurant makes breakfast.

Talk Together

Draw a picture of a **Key Word** for your partner to label.

worker

Add words to My Vocabulary Notebook.
NGReach.com

Read a Poem

✓ Look for rhyming words.

A new **day** is on its **way**.

rhyme

Reading Strategy

Ask questions as you read. What do trucks deliver to neighborhoods?

Delivery

by **Anastasia Suen**

illustrated by **Wade Zahares**

A new day is on its way.

Papers come one by one.

Boxes and cans come
in trucks and vans.

Unwrap it all for shelves on the wall.

173

wing

Wheels and wings carry
many things.

wheels

High and low, we come and go.

Trucks on roads carry loads.

loads

Trains speed by. Hello! Goodbye!

Containers wait at number eight.

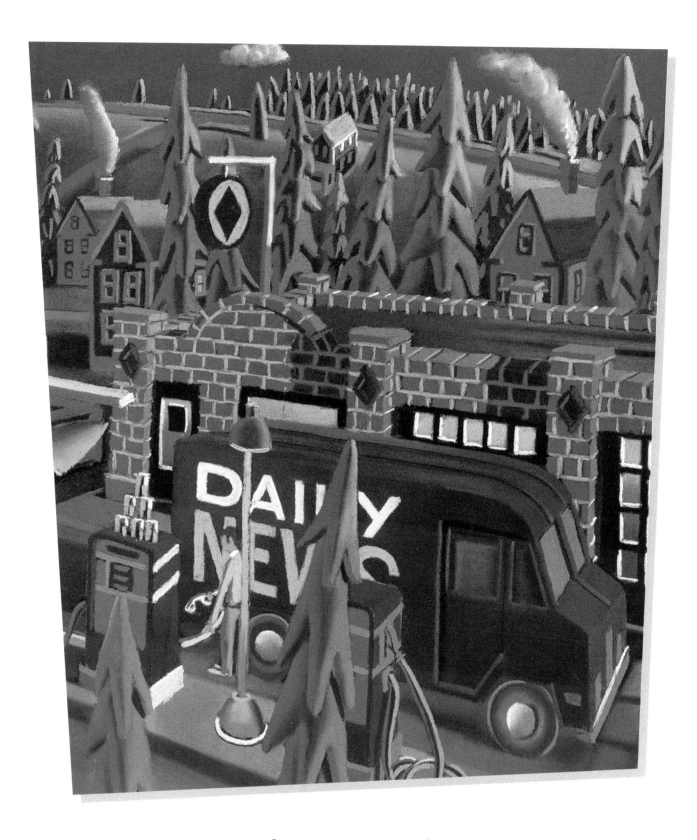

A new day is on its way.

Delivery! ❖

Meet the Author

Anastasia Suen

Anastasia Suen has written more than 100 books! She likes to write about real things.

Ms. Suen used to be a first grade teacher. Today she visits schools as an author.

▲ Anastasia Suen

Writer's Craft

Anastasia Suen uses verbs, such as **carry**, **speed**, and **wait**, in her poem. What are three other verbs you can use to describe deliveries?

Meet the Illustrator

Wade Zahares

Wade Zahares sells paintings and uses others in children's books.

Mr. Zahares had to practice to become a good artist. Now, he loves to paint whenever he can.

▲ Wade Zahares

Talk About It

1. How are boxes and cans **delivered**?

Boxes and cans are delivered ____ .

2. What would be different in the poem if there were no deliveries?

If there were no deliveries, ____ .

3. Which words in the poem rhyme?

____ and ____ rhyme.

Learn test-taking strategies.
NGReach.com

Write About It

Read this sentence. Which words rhyme?

Trucks on roads carry loads.

Write a new rhyme poem about a delivery.

____ deliver ____ .

Identify Details

How do goods get to **stores** in *Delivery*?

Idea Web

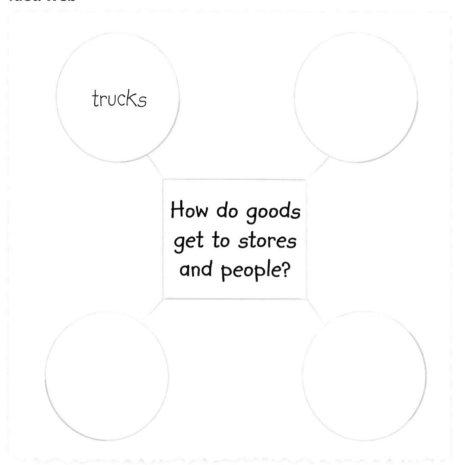

trucks

How do goods get to stores and people?

Use your web. Tell a partner what happens in *Delivery*.

A truck delivers goods to stores.

Identify Verbs

Carry and **ship** are **action verbs**. An action verb tells what someone or something does.

> The workers **carry** boxes.
> We **ship** goods on planes.

Try It Together

Read these sentences with a partner. Find the action verbs.

| I find a shirt at the store. |
| I ask my dad for the shirt. |
| I wear the new shirt home. |

Connect Across Texts You read about how people **deliver** things we need. Now read about how we pay for what we need.

Genre A **fact sheet** is nonfiction. This fact sheet gives facts about money.

Money

by
Heather Langer

Money can be paper.

one dollar bill

five dollar bill

ten dollar bill

twenty dollar bill

Money can be coins.

penny = one cent
1¢

nickel = five cents
5¢

dime = ten cents
10¢

quarter = twenty-five cents
25¢

People pay money for things they need.

People save money for things they want.

Compare Genres

How are *Delivery* and "Money" different?

Poem

Papers come one by one.

rhyming text

170

Fact Sheet

Money can be paper. **facts**

one dollar bill

five dollar bill

ten dollar bill

twenty dollar bill

Money can be coins.

penny = one cent
1¢

nickel = five cents
5¢

dime = ten cents
10¢

quarter = twenty-five cents
25¢

192

Talk Together

Think about what you read and learned. How do we get what we need and want?

Grammar and Spelling

Skills Trace: Verb *to be*   ↻ ◯
                 Verb *to have* ↻ ◯
              ▶ **Verbs *be* and *have***

Subject-Verb Agreement: be and *have*

Some **verbs** do not show action, such as **be** and **have**.

The truck **is** big. The truck **has** a flat tire. ⟨ | tells about one thing |

The boxes **are** heavy. The boxes **have** cans in them. ⟨ | tells about more than one thing |

Grammar Rules   Subject-Verb Agreement

be in present tense

To tell about one person, place, or thing, use **is**.

To tell about more than one, use **are**.

have in present tense

To tell about one person, place, or thing, use **has**.

To tell about more than one, use **have**.

Read a Sentence

Why is the verb *have* used in the sentence?

Three trucks **have** big wheels.

Write a Sentence

Write a sentence about one van. Use the verb *be*.

Write as a Family Member

Write a Thank You Letter ✏️

Think about a gift. Tell why the gift is special. Write a thank you letter for the gift.

May 1

Dear Aunt Olga,

   Thank you for the gift. I like it a lot. **I needed a backpack for my books**. **I wanted a pink one**. Where did you get it? I didn't see this style when I went to the store!

Love,

Sophie

Write the date and the person's name in the greeting.

Sophie tells why she **needed** and **wanted** the gift.

Write a closing and sign your name.

❶ Plan and Write

Work with a partner. Make a list of special gifts from family members. Pick one gift.

Write sentences to say thank you. Then write sentences that tell why you needed and wanted the gift.

❷ Check Your Work

Revise and edit your writing. Use this checklist.

❸ Finish and Share

Finish your thank you letter. Make sure you used the right greeting and closing.

Read the thank you letter to a friend. Speak clearly. Then give the letter to your family member who gave you the gift. Say *thank you* again!

Checklist
☑ Think about different verbs you can use. Can you use verbs that show action?
☑ Check your sentences. Do your subjects and verbs go together?
☑ Read your own work. Trace words with your finger. Check for backwords letters. Correct spelling errors.

I really like this gift! Thanks!

Share Your Ideas

Think about the things we use every day. How do we get what we need? Choose one of these ways to share your ideas about the **Big Question**.

Write It!

Make a T Chart

Make a T Chart with a partner. Write these headings: Things We Buy and Things That Are Free. Write three things for each side of the chart.

Things We Buy	Things That Are Free
shoes	friends
milk	sunshine
toys	the park

Talk About It!

Rhyming Fun
Read this poem. Have each person in the group add to it. Say a want or a need that rhymes with one of the words. Then make new rhymes.

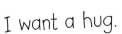

I want a hug.
I want a bug.
I need some food.
I need two shoes.

Do It!

Sort Wants and Needs
Cut pictures out of magazines of things you want and need. Make two folders. Label them. Put the pictures in the correct folder.

Want

Growing and Changing

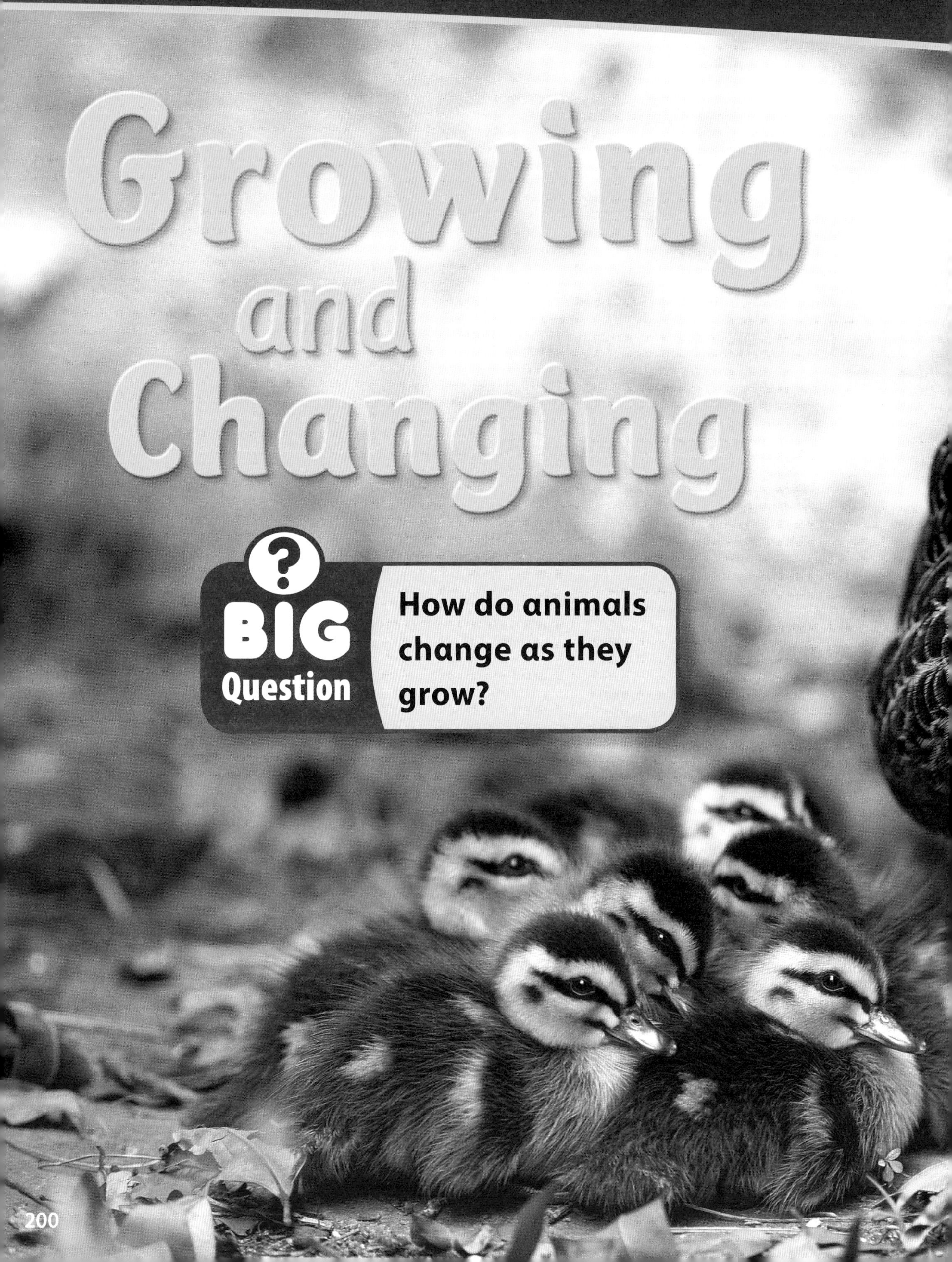

?

BIG

Question

How do animals change as they grow?

Share What You Know

Do It!

❶ **Draw** an animal you know as a baby, and then as an adult.

❷ **Tell** how the animal changed.

❸ **Show** what the baby can do. Show what the adult can do.

kitten

cat

Build Background: Watch a video about animals.
NGReach.com

Retell a Story

Listen and chant.

The Little Duckling

Chant (((MP3)))

First, the little duckling
Hatches in a nest.
Mother Duck says
He's not like the rest.

Next, the bigger ducklings
Don't want to play.
The little duckling cries.
Then, he runs away.

Finally, he's happy,
Swimming in the pond.
For now the little duckling
Has grown into a swan.

Key Words

How do animals grow and change?

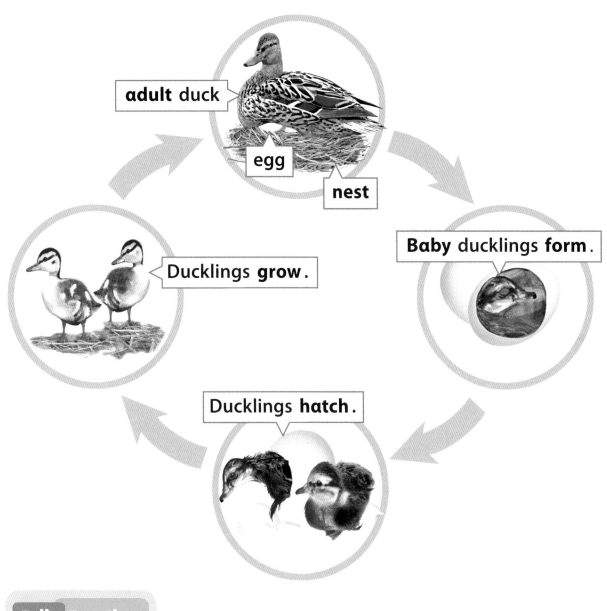

adult duck

egg

nest

Baby ducklings **form**.

Ducklings **grow**.

Ducklings **hatch**.

Talk Together

Look at the baby ducklings. How do they change as they grow? Use sequence words like first, next, and then.

Identify Plot

Begining-Middle-End Chart

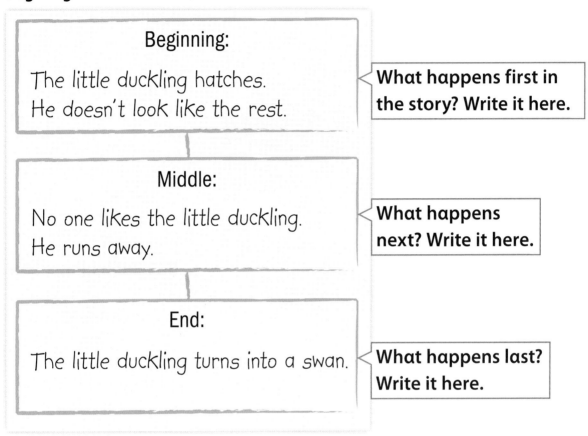

Beginning:

The little duckling hatches.
He doesn't look like the rest.

> **What happens first in the story? Write it here.**

Middle:

No one likes the little duckling.
He runs away.

> **What happens next? Write it here.**

End:

The little duckling turns into a swan.

> **What happens last? Write it here.**

Look for the plot as you listen and read.

Talk Together

Think of a story you know. Use a beginning-middle-end chart to write or draw the plot. Then use the chart to retell your story.

More Key Words

before

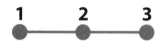

One comes **before** two.

inside

The books are **inside** the box.

shape

The **shape** of a ball is round.

size

My dad's shoes are not my **size**.

• time

Seven o'clock is the **time** we wake up.

Talk Together

Work with a partner to use each **Key Word** in a sentence.

It is time for ___ recess.

• High Frequency Word

Add words to My Vocabulary Notebook.
○ NGReach.com

Read a Story

Who is in the story?

Ruby

Mother Duck
and Father Duck

Rufus, Rory, Rosie, and Rebecca

Reading Strategy

As you read, look at the text and pictures to **determine what is important** in the story.

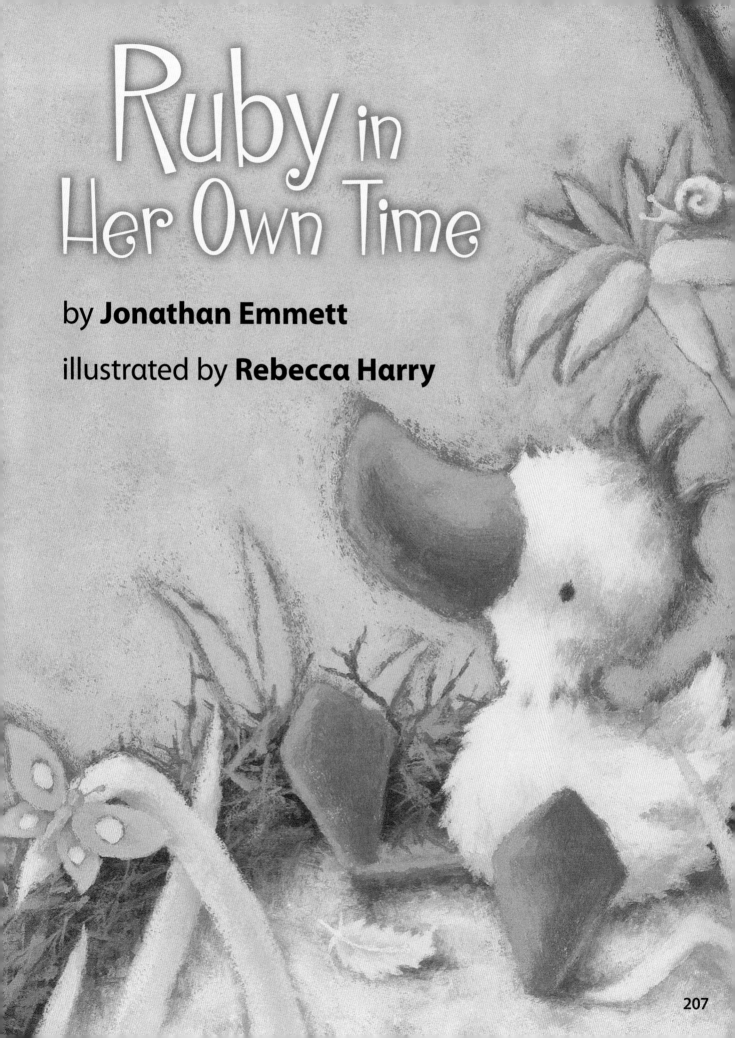

Ruby in Her Own Time

by **Jonathan Emmett**

illustrated by **Rebecca Harry**

Once upon a **time** upon a **nest**,
there lived two ducks.

A mother duck and a father duck.

There were five **eggs** in the nest.

Mother Duck sat upon the nest
all day,
and all night,

in wind,
and in rain.

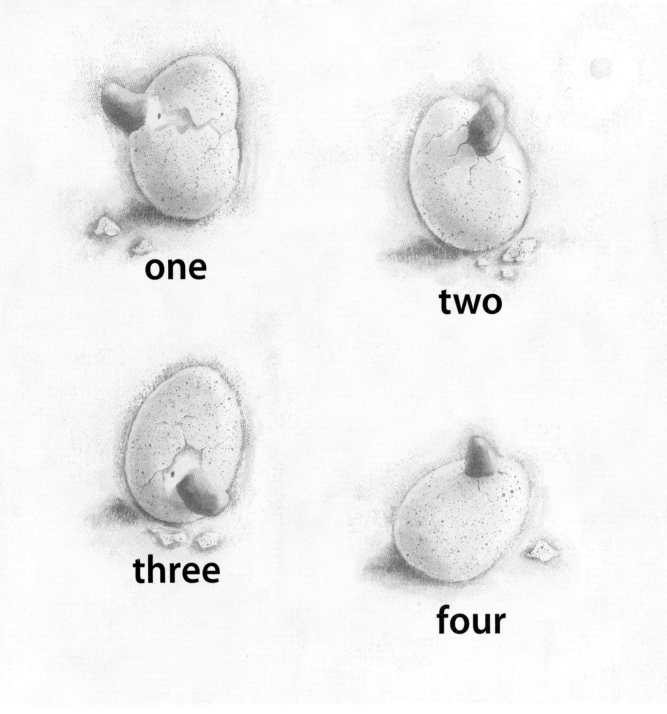

one

two

three

four

Then, one bright morning, the eggs began to **hatch**. Little beaks poked out into the sunlight.

one   two   three   four

"We'll call them Rufus, Rory, Rosie, and Rebecca," said Father Duck.

But the fifth egg did nothing.
"Will it ever hatch?" asked
Father Duck.

"It will," said Mother Duck,
"in its own time."

And it did.

"We'll call her Ruby," said
Mother Duck, "because she's
small and precious."

Rufus, Rory, Rosie, and Rebecca
ate whatever they were given.
But Ruby ate nothing.

"Will she ever eat?" asked
Father Duck.
"She will," said Mother Duck,
"in her own time."

And she did.

Rufus, Rory, Rosie, and Rebecca
swam everywhere.

But Ruby swam nowhere.

"Will she ever swim?" asked
Father Duck.
"She will," said Mother Duck,
"in her own time."

And she did.

Rufus, Rory, Rosie, and
Rebecca grew bigger.

And Ruby grew bigger, too.
And when Rufus, Rory, Rosie, and
Rebecca began to fly . . .

Ruby flew, too.

Rufus, Rory, Rosie, and Rebecca
flew far and wide. They flew up
among the trees.

But Ruby flew farther and wider.

She flew up above the trees.

She stretched out her beautiful
wings. She flew high among
the clouds.

Mother Duck and Father Duck
watched Ruby fly away.

"Will she ever come back?" asked Mother Duck.

"She will," said Father Duck, "in her own time."

And she did. ❖

Meet the Author
Jonathan Emmett

AWARD WINNER

Jonathan Emmett liked to read books and write stories when he was growing up.

Mr. Emmett gets lots of ideas from things that happen in real life. He keeps the ideas on his computer. That way, he won't forget to use them!

Writer's Craft

Find words that Jonathan Emmett repeats in the story. How does that make the story fun to read?

Talk About It

1. There are five **eggs**. Which egg is Ruby's?

    The ____ egg is Ruby's.

2. What does it mean that Ruby does things in her own **time**?

    It means ____ .

3. What happens after Ruby's wings **grow**?

    After Ruby's wings grow, she ____ .

Learn test-taking strategies.
NGReach.com

Write About It

Describe how Mother Duck and Father Duck feel about Ruby. How can you tell?

Mother Duck and Father Duck feel ____ . They ____ .

Identify Plot

What happens in this story? Use sequence words.

Begining-Middle-End Chart

> **Beginning:**
> First, Ruby hatches from an egg.

> **Middle:**

> **End:**

Use your chart to retell the story of *Ruby in Her Own Time*. Act out the events in order as you retell.

> Ruby is the last egg to hatch.

Use Context Clues

word clues	meaning

There were **five eggs** in the duck **nest**.	A **nest** is a place where ducks lay eggs.

Look at the words and sentences around a new word. You might find **word clues** to figure out the meaning.

Try It Together

Read the sentences. What does the word **hatch** mean? Talk about the word clues.

Then one bright morning, the eggs began to **hatch**. Little beaks poked out into the sunlight.

Connect Across Texts You read about how Ruby changes. Now read about how turtles change as they **grow** .

Genre A **science article** is nonfiction. This article gives facts about turtles.

Turtles: From Eggs to Ocean

by **Mariana Fuentes**

▲ Sea turtles live in many places around the world.

I am Mariana Fuentes. I study sea turtles.

▲ Turtles can lay over 100 eggs!

Sea turtles live in water, but they lay **eggs** on land.

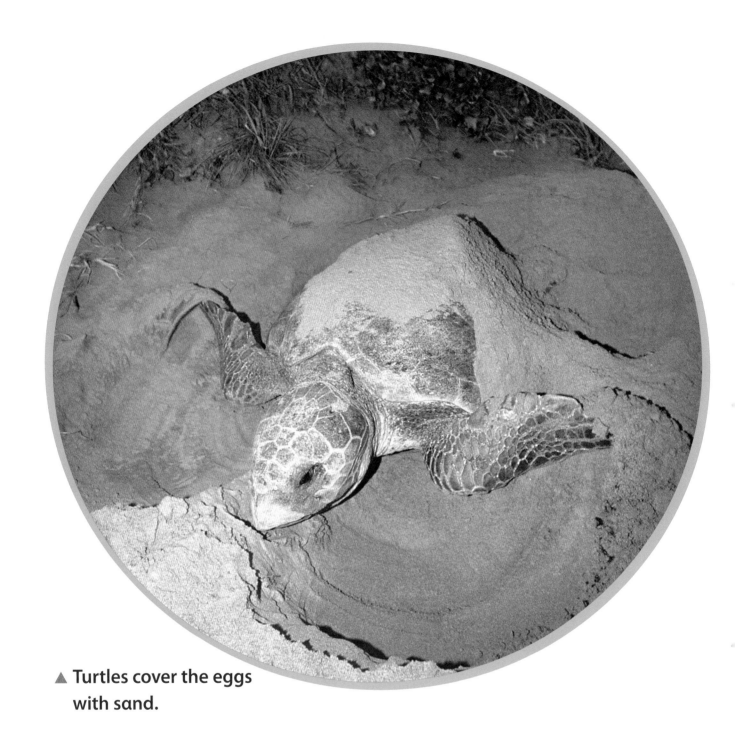

▲ Turtles cover the eggs
with sand.

Turtles make **nests** for their eggs
in sand. They make a hole, and lay
eggs. The eggs will **hatch** in about
two months.

▲ When the turtles hatch, they run to the ocean.

All the turtles hatch at the same
time. They will soon grow to
be **adult** turtles. They can live
to be 80 years old!

Compare Genres

How are *Ruby in Her Own Time* and "Turtles: From Eggs to Ocean" different?

Animal Fantasy

"Will she ever eat?" asked Father Duck.
"She will," said Mother Duck, "in her own time."

219

animals talk

Science Article

▲ Turtles can lay over 100 eggs!

Sea turtles live in water, but they lay **eggs** on land.

237

captions give
real information

Talk Together

Think about what you have read and learned.
How do animals change as they grow?

Grammar

Skills Trace: ▸ Singular Subject Pronouns: *I, you, it*
▸ Plural Subject Pronouns: *we, you, they*
▸ **Subject Pronoun Agreement**

Subject Pronouns

A **pronoun** can take the place of a **noun**.

Grammar Rules Subject Pronouns

Use **I** for yourself. Always use a capital letter for **I**.	**I** like turtles.
Use **he** for a male.	**Dad** reads about turtles. **He** reads about turtles.
Use **she** for a female.	**Mariana** sees real turtles. **She** sees real turtles.
Use **they** for more than one person.	**Lucy and José** see turtles. **They** see turtles.

Read a Sentence

Look at the noun. Which pronoun can take its place?

Amy draws a turtle.

Write a Sentence

What do you think about turtles? Write a sentence that starts with **I**. Read it to a partner.

Restate an Idea

Listen and sing.

Song ((MP3))

Change and Grow

Animals, animals
Change as they grow,
Change as they grow.
This is what I heard.
This is what I heard.
This is what I know.
This is what I know.

Insects, too, insects, too,
Change as they grow,
Change as they grow.
This is what I heard.
This is what I heard.
This is what I know.
This is what I know.

Tune: "Frère Jacques"

242

Key Words

See how the **insect** will **change** as it grows.

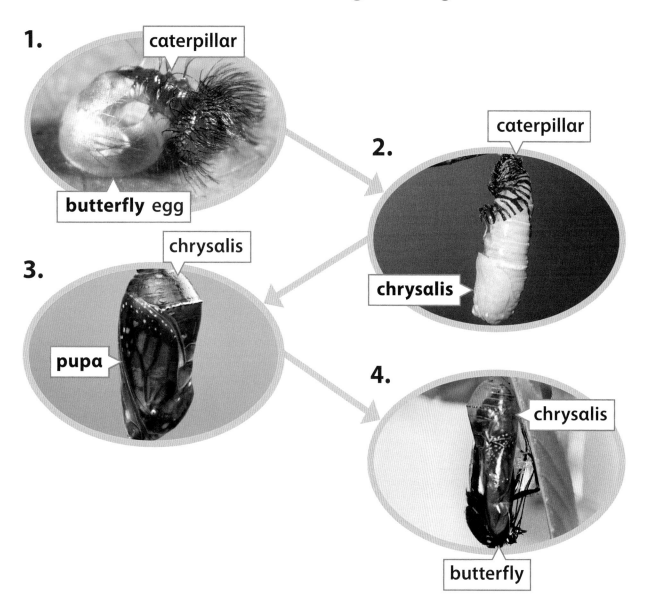

1. caterpillar

butterfly egg

2. caterpillar

chrysalis

3. chrysalis

pupa

4. chrysalis

butterfly

Talk Together

This insect changes as it grows. What do you know about how insects and animals change as they grow?

Identify Main Idea and Details

Main Idea and Details Chart

> **Main Idea:**
> Animals change as they grow.
>
> > **Detail:**
> > get bigger
> >
> > **Detail:**
> > start moving
> >
> > **Detail:**
> > change shape

Write the main idea here.

Write the details here.

Talk Together

Choose an animal. How does the animal **change** as it grows? Add the details to the chart.

More Key Words

attach

ring

You can **attach** keys to a ring.

born

This baby was **born** yesterday.

color

The **color** of the flower is red.

hard

The rock feels **hard**.

sequence

The letters are in order, or **sequence**.

Talk Together

Make word cards for each **Key Word**.

I was born
in August.

Add words to My Vocabulary Notebook.
NGReach.com

Read a Science Article

A **science article** is nonfiction. It tells about things that are real.

✓ Look for diagrams.

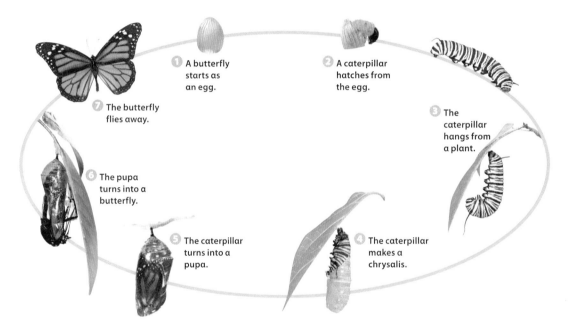

1. A butterfly starts as an egg.
2. A caterpillar hatches from the egg.
3. The caterpillar hangs from a plant.
4. The caterpillar makes a chrysalis.
5. The caterpillar turns into a pupa.
6. The pupa turns into a butterfly.
7. The butterfly flies away.

Diagrams show information.

Reading Strategy

As you read, **determine** importance.

What is the most important idea and why?

A Butterfly Is Born

by Fran Downey

butterfly

A **butterfly** sits on a plant.
She lays an egg.

egg

A butterfly egg is small.
It will hatch soon. Then
a **caterpillar** will come out.

caterpillar

The caterpillar is hungry. It eats the plant. The caterpillar grows.

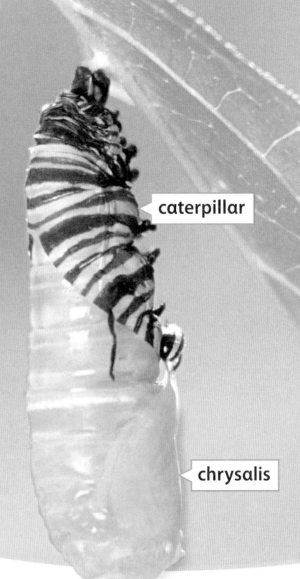

caterpillar

chrysalis

The caterpillar **changes**.
It hangs from a plant. It
makes a **chrysalis**.

chrysalis

The caterpillar stays in the chrysalis. The caterpillar turns into a **pupa**.

pupa

The pupa grows wings. It is a butterfly now. It comes out of the chrysalis.

chrysalis

butterfly

wet wings

The butterfly is tired. Its wings are wet. It rests and dries.

The butterfly flies away. ❖

A Butterfly Grows Up

1 A butterfly starts as an egg.

7 The butterfly flies away.

6 The pupa turns into a butterfly.

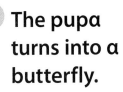

5 The caterpillar turns into a pupa.

② A caterpillar hatches from the egg.

③ The caterpillar hangs from a plant.

④ The caterpillar makes a chrysalis.

Talk About It

1. Why does the diagram, "A Butterfly Grows Up," make a circle?

It makes a circle to show _____ .

2. What does the **caterpillar** make to hang from a leaf?

The caterpillar makes a _____ .

3. What happens after the **pupa** grows wings?

After the pupa grows wings, it _____ .

Learn test-taking strategies.
NGReach.com

Write About It

Write the steps of how a butterfly is born.

1. _____
2. _____
3. _____
4. _____

Identify Main Idea and Details

Where does a butterfly come from?

Main Idea and Details Chart

Main Idea:
A caterpillar changes into a butterfly.

Detail:
hatches from an egg

Detail:

Detail:

Summarize what you learned about a butterfly's life. Use your main idea and details chart.

A caterpillar turns into a butterfly.

Use Context Clues

word clues	meaning

The caterpillar **changes**. It **turns into** a pupa.	When something **changes**, it turns into something different.

Look at the words and sentences around a new word. You might find **word clues** to figure out the meaning.

Try It Together

Look back at "A Butterfly Is Born." Find a sentence with the word **chrysalis**. Use word clues. Talk about the meaning of **chrysalis**.

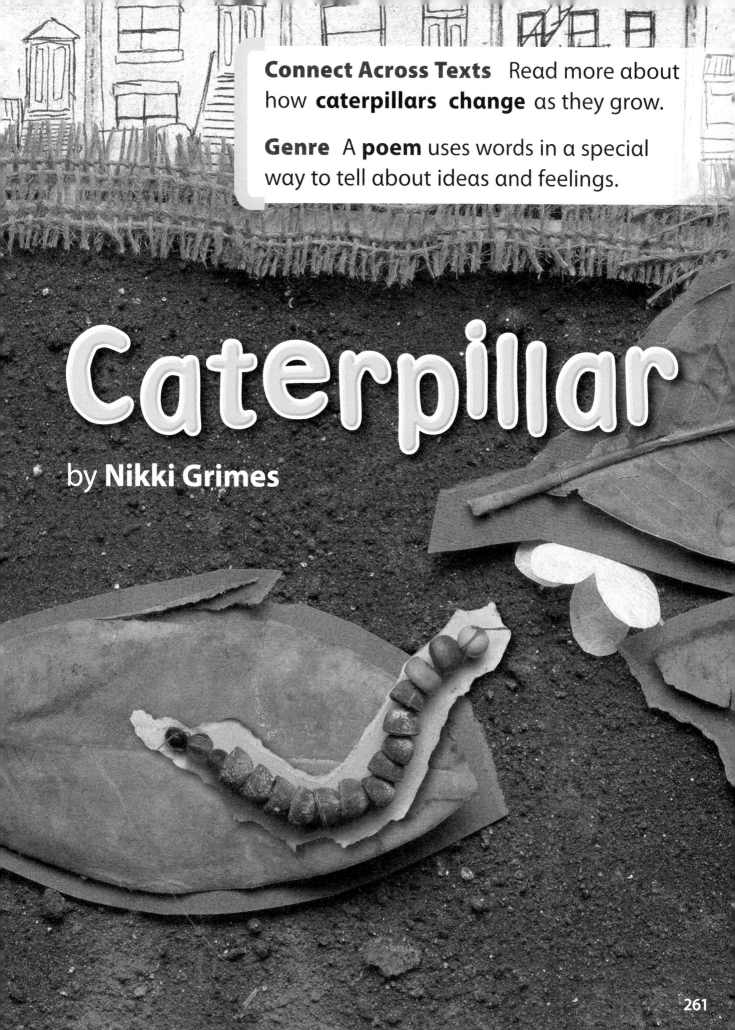

Connect Across Texts Read more about how **caterpillars change** as they grow.

Genre A **poem** uses words in a special way to tell about ideas and feelings.

Caterpillar

by **Nikki Grimes**

Caterpillar

The word wriggles in my pocket.
CATERPILLAR.
I reach for it, but it worms away crawling as fast as it can. I get down on my hands and knees to chase it.
Caterpillar, wait for me.
I haven't grown wings yet, either.
Soon, though!

Respond and Extend

Compare Genres

How is the information in "A Butterfly Is Born" and "Caterpillar" different?

Science Article

pupa

The pupa grows wings. It is a butterfly now. It comes out of the chrysalis.

253

real information

Poem

Caterpillar

The word wriggles in my pocket.
CATERPILLAR.
I reach for it, but it worms away crawling as fast as it can. I get down on my hands and knees to chase it.
Caterpillar, wait for me.
I haven't grown wings yet, either.
Soon, though!

263

information that is not real

Talk Together

Think about what you read and learned. How do things change as they grow?

Possessive Words

A **possessive word** tells who owns or has something.

This is **Marshall's** caterpillar.

This is **his** caterpillar.

Grammar Rules **Possessive Words**

Use **her** for one girl or one woman.		Butterflies land on **her** flowers.
Use **his** for one boy or one man.		Dad will use **his** garden tools.

Read a Sentence

Does the sentence use the correct possessive word? How do you know?

Nikki looked for her caterpillar.

Write a Sentence

Write a sentence using a possessive word to tell what a friend brings to school.

Write Like a Storyteller

Write a Story

Have you heard stories about when you were younger? Tell one of your stories about growing up. Write the story for a friend.

Big Bike Time

by Jayan Ramahan

It was time for me to ride a big bike.

beginning > First, I sat on the seat. Dad held the bike.

middle > Next, I started to pedal. Dad held the bike.

end > Last, I rode away. Dad watched me go!

Stories have a title and an author.

266

① Plan and Write

Talk with a partner about stories you heard from your family. Pick one story. Tell your partner what happened first, next, and last.

Write your ideas. Then write the beginning, middle, and end of the story.

② Check Your Work

Revise and edit your writing. Use this checklist.

Checklist

- ☑ Can you repeat a word to make your story more fun to read?
- ☑ Check your sentences. Did you use a capital letter for the pronoun I?
- ☑ Read your story aloud. Check for words that sound alike. Correct spelling errors.

③ Finish and Share

Finish your story. Write each sentence neatly. Leave spaces between words.

Read your story. Be a good listener.

I learned how to play soccer from my dad.

Share Your Ideas

Think about how animals change as they grow. Choose one of these ways to share your ideas about the **Big Question**.

Write It! ✏️

Draw a Sequence Chain

Draw a sequence chain that shows how an animal grows. Show three steps in the sequence. Number each step in order.

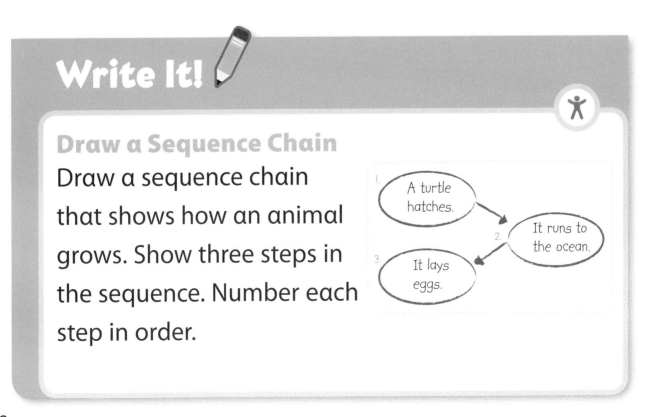

1. A turtle hatches.
2. It runs to the ocean.
3. It lays eggs.

Talk About It!

Question and Answer Game

Point to diagrams and photos in the unit. Ask **before and after** questions about sequence.

Have your partner answer **before** or **after**.

Does Ruby fly **before** or **after** she is born?

After!

Do It!

Show the Order

Draw images of a caterpillar, a butterfly, and a pupa inside of a chrysalis. Give three students the drawings. Take turns putting the students in order to show how a caterpillar changes into a butterfly.

a
b
c
d
e
f
g
h
i
j
k
l
m
n
o
p
q
r
s
t
u
v
w
x
y
z

A

adult

*My dad is an **adult**.*

alive

plant

pot

*A plant is **alive**. A pot is not.*

attach

ring

key

*You can **attach** keys to a ring.*

B

baby

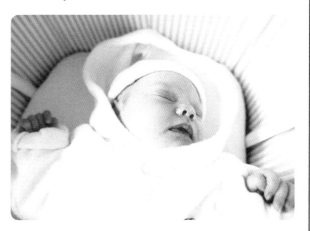

*The **baby** is sleeping.*

before

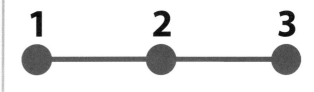

1   2   3

*One comes **before** two.*

born

*This baby was **born** yesterday.*

breathe

*She likes to **breathe** the cold air.*

bring

*I **bring** my backpack with me.*

bud

*The flower **bud** will bloom in a few days.*

business

*My father owns a flower **business**.*

butterfly

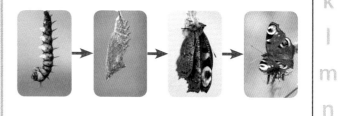

*The **butterfly** used to be a caterpillar.*

buy

*They **buy** milk at the store.*

care

I **care** for the plants.

caterpillar

This **caterpillar** is eating a leaf.

celebrate

Grandma **celebrates** her birthday.

change

The water will **change** into ice if you put it in the freezer.

chrysalis

The caterpillar changes inside the **chrysalis**.

color

The **color** of the flower is red.

count

*She **counts** how much money she saved.*

D

delivery

*Our mail **delivery** is late today.*

drink

*Orange juice is my favorite **drink**.*

E

earn

*The boy worked to **earn** money.*

eat

*She **eats** all her salad!*

egg

*The chick is hatching from the **egg**.*

a
b
c
d
e
f
g
h
i
j
k
l
m
n
o
p
q
r
s
t
u
v
w
x
y
z

energy

*Swimming takes a lot of **energy**.*

exercise

*My heart beats fast when I **exercise**.*

extended family

*This **extended family** is spending time together.*

F

factory

*This **factory** makes candy!*

family

*There are five people in my **family**.*

family member

*My uncle is a **family member**, but he does not live with us.*

flower

*This **flower** is a kind of daisy.*

food

*My family likes many kinds of **food**.*

form

*Chicks **form** inside of eggs until they are ready to hatch.*

fun

*Floating in the pool is **fun**!*

goods

*Stores sell these **goods**.*

group

*A **group** has more than two items.*

275

grow

*If you give a plant plenty of water, it will **grow** bigger.*

hard

*The rock feels **hard**.*

hatch

*Snakes **hatch** out of eggs, much like birds do.*

health

*Brushing your teeth is good for your **health**.*

height

*This basketball player's **height** is seven feet.*

help

*I **help** fold the clothes.*

holiday

*Our favorite **holiday** is the Fourth of July!*

home

*Your **home** is where you live with your family. There are many different kinds of homes.*

idea

*Lori's **idea** is to go to the zoo.*

insect

*A ladybug is a type of **insect**.*

inside

*Books are **inside** this box.*

job

My grandpa has a **job** at the grocery store.

leaf

This **leaf** is bright green.

length

The **length** of the carrot is 7 inches.

light

The **light** is bright enough to read the book.

living

The goldfish is a **living** thing. The bowl is not.

market

They are buying tomatoes at the **market**.

meal

*We eat our **meals** together.*

money

*He has a lot of **money**.*

move

*A sloth **moves** very slowly.*

needs

*Food and clothing are **needs**.*

neighborhood

*A parade came through our **neighborhood**.*

nest

*The bird is flying back to its **nest**.*

nonliving

*Rocks and water are **nonliving** things.*

parents

*My **parents** like to cook with me.*

petal

*This flower has yellow and pink **petals**.*

place

*This school is a big **place**.*

play

*We **play** a game together.*

project

*I am so proud of my science fair **project**.*

pupa

*This **pupa** will soon be an adult moth.*

sell

*He **sells** flowers at the market.*

ready

*The runner is **ready** to race.*

sequence

*The letters are in order, or **sequence**.*

seed

*A tiny apple **seed**, can grow into a big apple tree!*

service

*A **service** is work someone does for money, such as cutting hair.*

shape

*The **shape** of a ball is round.*

share

*We **share** the popcorn.*

ship

*He **ships** the present for my grandma.*

shop

*I like to **shop** at the bookstore.*

size

*My dad's shoes are not my **size**.*

special

*Today is her **special** day.*

store

*We are shopping at the **store**.*

sun

*The **sun** is very bright today.*

time

*Seven o'clock is the **time** we wake up.*

together

*We can win if we all work **together**.*

trip

*We take a **trip** in our car.*

visit

*I like it when my grandparents come for a **visit**.*

wants

*Toys and games are **wants**.*

worker

*A **worker** at the restaurant makes lunch.*

world

*This is how our **world** looks from space.*

Index

Index, *continued*

I

Ideas

see Express ideas, Speaking, express ideas

K

Key words

see Vocabulary

L

Language Functions

see Speaking, Listening

Listening

ask for and give information 5, 6, 23, 33, 65, 70, 87, 97, 118, 120, 155, 156, 163, 164, 188, 190, 233, 234, 243, 244, 258

collaborate with peers 30, 60, 61, 63, 65, 88, 92, 96, 120, 126, 129, 131, 136, 156, 160, 164, 165, 190, 194, 197, 234, 240, 244, 245, 260, 264, 267

comprehend spoken language 5, 6, 30, 33, 34, 61, 63, 65, 69, 70, 92, 93, 95, 96, 120, 126, 131, 135, 160, 161, 163, 189, 194, 203, 240, 241, 264, 269

monitor understanding of spoken language 70, 120, 131, 137, 163, 260, 269

to discussions 5, 6, 30, 33, 34, 61, 63, 65, 70, 92, 120, 126, 136, 160, 164, 194, 240, 260, 264

to instructions

following 5, 6, 7, 23, 30, 33, 34, 35, 60, 61, 63, 65, 69, 70, 87, 88, 92, 95, 96, 97, 118, 119, 120, 126, 131, 135, 136, 155, 156, 160, 163, 164, 165, 188, 189, 190, 194, 199, 204, 203, 233, 234, 240, 243, 244, 245, 258, 259, 260, 264, 269

to language structures 62, 129, 190, 197, 199, 241, 267

to media

audio tape

CD ROM

DVD

MP3 4, 33, 68, 94, 134, 162, 202, 242

video 3, 67, 133, 201

to messages 67

to speakers

asking questions 70

being attentive 5, 6, 7, 23, 30, 33, 34, 35, 61, 63, 65, 69, 70, 87, 88, 92, 95, 96, 97, 118, 119, 120, 126, 129, 131, 135, 136, 155, 156, 160, 163, 164, 165, 188, 189, 190, 194, 197, 199, 203, 204, 233, 234, 240, 243, 244, 245, 258, 259, 260, 264, 267, 269

making comments 67, 120, 131

to stories 95, 96, 266, 267

to vocabulary 5, 7, 33, 35, 69, 70, 71, 95, 97, 135, 137, 163, 165, 203, 205, 243, 245

Index, continued

Index of Authors

Index of Illustrators

Acknowledgments, continued

Text Credits

Unit One

Capstone Press: Excerpt from *Families in Many Cultures* by Heather Adamson. Copyright © by Capstone Press. Reprinted by permission of Capstone Press. All rights reserved.

HarperCollins Children's Books: Adaptation of *Papa and Me* by Arthur Dorros, illustrated by Rudy Gutierrez. Text copyright © 2008 by Arthur Dorros, illustrations © 2008 by Rudy Gutierrez. Reprinted by permission of HarperCollins Children's Books, a division of HarperCollins Publishers.

Unit Two

Picture Window Books: Excerpt from *Are You Living?* by Linda Purdie Salas. Copyright © 2009 by Picture Window Books. Reprinted by permission of Picture Window Books. All rights reserved.

Macmillan/McGraw Hill: "The Daisy" originally published as "La Margarita" by Lada Kratky. Copyright © 1993 by Macmillan. Reprinted by arrangement with Macmillan/McGraw Hill.

Unit Three

Capstone Global Library Limited: Excerpt from *Our Global Community: Markets* by Cassie Mayer. Copyright © 2007 by Heinemann Library. Reprinted under license from Capstone Global Library Limited. All rights reserved.

Anastasia Suen and Studio Goodwin Sturges: Excerpt from *Delivery* by Anastasia Suen, illustrated by Wade Zahares. Text copyright © 1999 by Anastasia Suen. Reprinted by permission of the author. Illustrations copyright © 1999 by Wade Zaharas. Reprinted by permission of Studio Goodwin Sturges on behalf of the artist.

Unit Four

Scholastic, Inc.: Adaptation of *Ruby in Her Time* by Jonathan Emmett, illustrated by Rebecca Harry. Text copyright © 2004 by Jonathan Emmett, illustrations © 2004 by Rebecca Harry. Reprinted by permission of Scholastic Inc.

Houghton Mifflin Harcourt: "Caterpillar," by Nikki Grimes, illustrated by Javaka Steptoe, from *A Pocketful of Poems.* Copyright © 2001 by Nikki Grimes. Illustrations © 2001 by Javaka Steptoe. Reprinted by permission of Clarion Books, an imprint of Houghton Mifflin Harcourt Publishing Company. All rights reserved.

NATIONAL GEOGRAPHIC SCHOOL PUBLISHING

National Geographic School Publishing gratefully acknowledges the contributions of the following National Geographic Explorers to our program and to our planet:

Josh Thorne, 2008 National Geographic Emerging Explorer
Michael Fay, National Geographic Explorer-in-Residence
Cid Simoes and Paola Segura, 2008 National Geographic Emerging Explorers
Mariana Fuentes, National Geographic Grantee
Greg Marshall, National Geographic Scientist
Tim Samaras, 2005 National Geographic Emerging Explorer
Constance Adams, 2005 National Geographic Emerging Explorer
Michael DiSpezio, National Geographic Presenter

Photographic Credits

iv (tc) Simon Marcus/Corbis. v (tl) Michael Christopher Brown/National Geographic Image Collection. vi (tl) Jeff Greenberg/Alamy Images. vii (tl) Stephen Frink Collection/Alamy Images. ix (tr) Simon Marcus/Corbis. 2-3 (bg) Dean Mitchell/Alamy Images. 3 (inset) Liz Garza Williams/Hampton-Brown/National Geographic School Publishing. 5 Photodisc/Getty Images. 6 Digital Vision/Getty Images. 7 (bl) Orange Line Media/Shutterstock. (br) Stockbyte/Getty Images. (tc) Corbis Super RF/Alamy Images. (tl) Alistair Berg/Digital Vision/Jupiterimages. (tr) Glenda Powers/iStockphoto. 8 (l) GoGo Images Corporation/Alamy Images. (r) Studio DL/Corbis. 8-9 (bg) David Young-Wolff/Alamy Images. 10 Sean Sprague/Sprague Photo Stock. 12 GoGo Images Corporation/Alamy Images. 13 Corbis Premium RF/Alamy Images. 14 Fancy/Alamy Images. 15 Studio DL/Corbis. 16 Marc Edwards/Peter Arnold, Inc. 17 Simon Marcus/Corbis. 18 Blend Images/Alamy Images. 19 Cliff Parnell/iStockphoto. 20-21 Corbis. 22 Monkey Business Images/Shutterstock. 23 Image Source/Jupiterimages. 24 David Young-Wolff/Alamy Images. 25 4Real. 26 (b) Aaron Huey/4Real. (t) 4Real. 27 (b) Penelopy Kalopisi-Kennedy/4Real. (t) Melahnie Moodie/4Real. 28 (l) Carolina for Kibera. 28-29 (bg) Photos.com/Jupiterimages. (c) 4Real. 29 (r) Melahnie Moodie/4Real. 30 (bg) Photos.com/Jupiterimages. (c) 4Real. (l) Marc Edwards/Peter Arnold, Inc. (r) Melahnie Moodie/4Real. 31 (bl) PhotoDisc/Getty Images. (blc) PhotoDisc/Getty Images. (br) RTimages/Shutterstock. (brc) RTimages/Shutterstock. (tl) PhotoDisc/Getty Images. (tr) RTimages/Shutterstock. 33 (b) Monkey Business Images/Shutterstock. (t) A. Ramey/PhotoEdit. 34 Purestock/Alamy Images. 35 (bl) Pixland/Jupiterimages. (br) Ronnie Kaufman/Blend Images/Jupiterimages. (tcl) iodrakon/iStockphoto. (tcr) lillisphotography/iStockphoto. (tl) C Squared Studios/Photodisc/Getty Images. (tr) Sarah Hadley/Alamy Images. 53 Alex Dorros. 55 MIXA/Alamy Images. 57 DigitalStock/Corbis. 58-59 (bg) DigitalStock/Corbis. 59 (inset) DigitalStock/Corbis. 60 DigitalStock/Corbis. 61 PhotoDisc/Getty Images. 62 (b) Ariel Skelley/Blend Images/Jupiterimages. (c) Alex Kotlov/iStockphoto. (t) Masterfile. 64 Dean Mitchell/Alamy Images. 65 rphotos/iStockphoto. 66-67 (bg) Aflo/Alamy Images. 67 (inset) Liz Garza Williams/Hampton-Brown/National Geographic School Publishing. 70 (b) Mike Flippo/Shutterstock. (t) Liz Garza Williams/Hampton-Brown/National Geographic School Publishing. 71 (bl) Christina Kennedy/Alamy Images. (br) Blend Images/Alamy Images. (tc) Comstock/Jupiterimages. (tl) Elena Butinova/Shutterstock. (tr) Juice/Jupiterimages. 87 (l) Liz Garza Williams/Hampton-Brown/National Geographic School Publishing. (r) Liz Garza Williams/Hampton-Brown/National Geographic School Publishing. 88 (bcr) Robert Pickett/Papilio/Alamy Images. (bl) PhotoDisc/Getty Images. (br) Michael Melford/National Geographic Image Collection. (cl) G.K. & Vikki Hart/Photodisc/Getty Images. (rcc) Photodisc/Getty Images. (tcr) MetaTools. (tl) SuperStock. (tr) Stockbyte/Getty Images. 89 MIXA/Alamy Images. 90 (b) PhotoDisc/Getty Images. (tl) Bold Stock/Unlisted Images. (tr) Creatas/Jupiterimages. 91 (b) ethylalkohol/Shutterstock. (tl) Creatas/Jupiterimages. (tr) Daniel Valla FRPS/Alamy Images. 92 (b) PhotoDisc/Getty Images. (tl) Bold Stock/Unlisted Images. (tr) Creatas/Jupiterimages. 93 (b) Roman Sigaev/Shutterstock. (c) N.Minton/Shutterstock. (t) Creatas/Jupiterimages. 97 (bl) Corbis Premium RF/Alamy Images. (br) James Pauls/iStockphoto. (tcl) Stockbyte/Getty Images. (tcr) Getty Images. (tl) Julián Rovagnati/Shutterstock. (tr) markomatovic/Shutterstock. 117 Lada Kratky. 119 Liz Garza Williams/Hampton-

Brown/National Geographic School Publishing. 121 (bg) DigitalStock/Corbis. (inset) George Steinmetz/National Geographic Image Collection. 122 Michael Christopher Brown/National Geographic Image Collection. 123 Michael Nichols/National Geographic Image Collection. 124-125 (bg) James P. Blair/National Geographic Image Collection. 126 Michael Nichols/National Geographic Image Collection. 127 Whitechild/Shutterstock. 129 Liz Garza Williams/Hampton-Brown/National Geographic School Publishing. 130 Aflo/Alamy Images. 131 (b) Rick Holcomb/Hampton-Brown/National Geographic School Publishing. (t) Liz Garza Williams/Hampton-Brown/National Geographic School Publishing. 132-133 (bg) Andrjuss/Shutterstock. 133 (inset) Liz Garza Williams/Hampton-Brown/National Geographic School Publishing. 136 (bl) Jeffrey Coolidge/Getty Images. (blc) Ralph Wachler/Bon Appetit/Alamy Images. (br) Blend Images/Alamy Images. (brc) Patrick Byrd/Alamy Images. (tcl) Spirit/Corbis. (tl) David Young-Wolff/PhotoEdit. (tr) Glowimages/Getty Images. (trc) Steve Skjold/Alamy Images. 137 (bl) Monkey Business Images/Shutterstock. (br) Peter Hansen/Shutterstock. (tcb) Mackey Creations/Shutterstock. (tcr) Premier Edition Image Library/Superstock. (tcr) PhotoDisc/Getty Images. (tl) BlueMoon Stock/Alamy Images. (tr) Jeffrey Smith/iStockphoto. 138 (inset) DBURKE/Alamy Images. 138-139 (bg) Tibor Bognár/Corbis. 140 Blend Images/Alamy Images. 141 Jeremy Richards/Shutterstock. 142 Steve McCurry/National Geographic Image Collection. 143 The Image Bank/Gary John Norman/Getty Images. 144 PhotoDisc/Getty Images. 145 Jeff Greenberg/Alamy Images. 146 Medioimages/Photodisc/Getty Images. 147 Layne Kennedy/Corbis. 148 DBURKE/Alamy Images. 149 adam eastland/Alamy Images. 150 Sherri R. Camp/Shutterstock. 151 PhotoDisc/Getty Images. 152 Jon Arnold Images Ltd/Alamy Images. 153 Robert Frerck/Odyssey Productions, Chicago. 154 Jeff Greenberg/Alamy Images. 155 picturepartners/Shutterstock. 156 Alex Segre/Alamy Images. 157 waldhaeusl com/Bildagentur Waldhaeusl/age fotostock. 158 (b) Paulo Fridman/Corbis. (t) Victor Sanchez de Fuentes. 158-159 (bg) Ricardo Azoury/iStockphoto. 159 (b) Picture Contact/Alamy Images. (t) Stephen Shepherd/Alamy Images. 160 (bg) Ricardo Azoury/iStockphoto. (br) Paulo Fridman/Corbis. (l) Blend Images/Alamy Images. (tr) Victor Sanchez de Fuentes. 164 Digifoto Diamond/Alamy Images. 165 (bl) Steven Bushong/iStockphoto. (br) PhotoDisc/Getty Images. (tc) Corbis/Jupiterimages. (tl) Floresco Productions/Cultura/Jupiterimages. (tr) Brand X/Jupiterimages/Alamy Images. 186 Cecil Stringfellow/Anastasia Suen. 187 Wade Zahares. 188 manley620/iStockphoto. 189 Liz Garza Williams/Hampton-Brown/National Geographic School Publishing. 191 Purestock/Alamy Images. 192 (bcl) Artville. (bcr) Artville. (bg) Idamini/Alamy Images. (bl) Artville. (br) Artville. (tcl) Ilene MacDonald/Alamy Images. (tcr) Ilene MacDonald/Alamy Images. (tl) Artville. (tr) Ilene MacDonald/Alamy Images. 193 (bl) M. Dykstra/Shutterstock. (br) Arvind Balaraman/Shutterstock. (t) David Young-Wolff/PhotoEdit. 194 (bcl) Artville. (bcr) Artville. (bg) Idamini/Alamy Images. (bl) Artville. (br) Artville. (tcl) Ilene MacDonald/Alamy Images. (tcr) Ilene MacDonald/Alamy Images. (tl) Artville. (tr) Ilene MacDonald/Alamy Images. 196 PhotoDisc/Getty Images. 197 Liz Garza Williams/Hampton-Brown/National Geographic School Publishing. 198 Andrjuss/Shutterstock. 200-201 (bg) Philip Quirk/Photolibrary. 201 (inset) Liz Garza Williams/Hampton-Brown/National Geographic School Publishing. 205 (bl) Geoff Tipton/iStockphoto. (br) Lorraine Kourafas/Shutterstock. (tl) iStockphoto. (tr) Aflo/Jupiterimages. 233 Marilyn Nieves/iStockphoto. 235 Stephen Frink Collection/Alamy Images. 236 Joshua Cinner. 237 Matthew Maran/Nature Picture Library. 238 Moodboard/

Illustrator Credits

California Common Core State Standards

SE Pages	Lesson	Code	Standard
2-3	**Unit Launch:** Share What You Know		With prompting and support, read prose and poetry of appropriate complexity for grade 1.
		CA CC.1.Rlit.10.a	**Activate prior knowledge related to the information and events in a text. CA**
		CA CC.1.SL.4	Describe people, places, things, and events with relevant details, expressing ideas and feelings clearly.
		CA CC.1.SL.5	Add drawings or other visual displays to descriptions when appropriate to clarify ideas, thoughts, and feelings.
4	**Part 1:** Language: Describe	CA CC.1.SL.4	Describe people, places, things, and events with relevant details, expressing ideas and feelings clearly.
		CA CC.1.SL.4.a	**Memorize and recite poems, rhymes, and songs with expression. CA**
5	**Social Studies Vocabulary:** Key Words	CA CC.1.L.4.a	Determine or clarify the meaning of unknown and multiple-meaning words and phrases based on *grade 1 reading and content,* choosing flexibly from an array of strategies.
			Use sentence-level context as a clue to the meaning of a word or phrase.
6	**Thinking Map:** Organize Ideas		With prompting and support, read informational texts appropriately complex for grade 1.
		CA CC.1.Rinf.10.a	**Activate prior knowledge related to the information and events in a text. CA**
		CA CC.1.SL.4	Describe people, places, things, and events with relevant details, expressing ideas and feelings clearly.
7	**Academic Vocabulary:** More Key Words		Determine or clarify the meaning of unknown and multiple-meaning words and phrases based on *grade 1 reading and content,* choosing flexibly from an array of strategies.
		CA CC.1.L.4.a	Use sentence-level context as a clue to the meaning of a word or phrase.
		CA CC.1.L.5.c	Identify real-life connections between words and their use (e.g., note places at home that are *cozy*).
8	**Selection 1 Preview:** Read a Photo Book	CA CC.1.Rinf.7	Use the illustrations and details in a text to describe its key ideas.
			Read with sufficient accuracy and fluency to support comprehension.
		CA CC.1.Rfou.4.a	Read on-level text with purpose and understanding.
9-21	**Selection 1:** Photo Book Families in Many Cultures	CA CC.1.Rinf.10	With prompting and support, read informational texts appropriately complex for grade 1.

California Common Core State Standards, *continued*

SE Pages	Lesson	Code	Standard
22	**Think and Respond:** Talk About It	CA CC.1.Rinf.2	Identify the main topic and retell key details of a text.
			Read with sufficient accuracy and fluency to support comprehension.
		CA CC.1.Rfou.4.a	Read on-level text with purpose and understanding.
		CA CC.1.SL.6	Produce complete sentences when appropriate to task and situation. (See grade 1 Language standards 1 and 3 for specific expectations.)
		CA CC.1.L.6	Use words and phrases acquired through conversations, reading and being read to, and responding to texts, including using frequently occurring conjunctions to signal simple relationships (e.g., *because*).
	Think and Respond: Write About It	CA CC.1.W.8	With guidance and support from adults, recall information from experiences or gather information from provided sources to answer a question.
		CA CC.1.L.6	Use words and phrases acquired through conversations, reading and being read to, and responding to texts, including using frequently occurring conjunctions to signal simple relationships (e.g., *because*).
23	**Reread and Retell:** Organize Ideas	CA CC.1.Rinf.2	Identify the main topic and retell key details of a text.
		CA CC.1.Rinf.7	Use the illustrations and details in a text to describe its key ideas.
		CA CC.1.W.8	With guidance and support from adults, recall information from experiences or gather information from provided sources to answer a question.
		CA CC.1.SL.1	Participate in collaborative conversations with diverse partners about *grade 1 topics and texts* with peers and adults in small and larger groups.
24	**Word Work:** Identify Nouns		Demonstrate command of the conventions of standard English grammar and usage when writing or speaking.
		CA CC.1.L.1.b	Use common, proper, and possessive nouns.
25-29	**Selection 2:** Magazine Article The World Is Your Family	CA CC.1.Rinf.10	With prompting and support, read informational texts appropriately complex for grade 1.
30	**Respond and Extend:** Compare Author's Purpose	CA CC.1.Rinf.2	Identify the main topic and retell key details of a text.
		CA CC.1.Rinf.9	Identify basic similarities in and differences between two texts on the same topic (e.g., in illustrations, descriptions, or procedures).
31	**Grammar and Spelling:** Plural Nouns		Demonstrate command of the conventions of standard English grammar and usage when writing or speaking.
		CA CC.1.L.1.b	Use common, proper, and possessive nouns.
			Determine or clarify the meaning of unknown and multiple-meaning words and phrases based on *grade 1 reading and content,* choosing flexibly from an array of strategies.
		CA CC.1.L.4.c	Identify frequently occurring root words (e.g., *look*) and their inflectional forms (e.g., *looks, looked, looking*).

SE Pages	Lesson	Code	Standard
32	**Part 2:** Language: Give Information	CA CC.1.SL.4	Describe people, places, things, and events with relevant details, expressing ideas and feelings clearly.
		CA CC.1.SL.4.a	**Memorize and recite poems, rhymes, and songs with expression. CA**
33	**Social Studies Vocabulary:** Key Words	CA CC.1.SL.1	Participate in collaborative conversations with diverse partners about *grade 1 topics and texts* with peers and adults in small and larger groups.
			Determine or clarify the meaning of unknown and multiple-meaning words and phrases based on *grade 1 reading and content,* choosing flexibly from an array of strategies.
		CA CC.1.L.4.a	Use sentence-level context as a clue to the meaning of a word or phrase.
34	**Thinking Map:** Identify Setting	CA CC.1.W.8	With guidance and support from adults, recall information from experiences or gather information from provided sources to answer a question.
		CA CC.1.SL.4	Describe people, places, things, and events with relevant details, expressing ideas and feelings clearly.
		CA CC.1.SL.5	Add drawings or other visual displays to descriptions when appropriate to clarify ideas, thoughts, and feelings.
35	**Academic Vocabulary:** More Key Words		Know and apply grade-level phonics and word analysis skills in decoding words **both in isolation and in text. CA**
		CA CC.1.Rfou.3.d	Use knowledge that every syllable must have a vowel sound to determine the number of syllables in a printed word.
			Determine or clarify the meaning of unknown and multiple-meaning words and phrases based on *grade 1 reading and content,* choosing flexibly from an array of strategies.
		CA CC.1.L.4.a	Use sentence-level context as a clue to the meaning of a word or phrase.
36	**Selection 1 Preview:** Read a Story	CA CC.1.Rlit.7	Use illustrations and details in a story to describe its characters, setting, or events.
			With prompting and support, read prose and poetry of appropriate complexity for grade 1.
		CA CC.1.Rlit.10.a	**Activate prior knowledge related to the information and events in a text. CA**
37-52	**Selection 1:** Story Papá and Me	CA CC.1.Rlit.10	With prompting and support, read prose and poetry of appropriate complexity for grade 1.
53	**Meet the Author:** Writer's Craft	CA CC.1.Rlit.7	Use illustrations and details in a story to describe its characters, setting, or events.
		CA CC.1.W.8	With guidance and support from adults, recall information from experiences or gather information from provided sources to answer a question.

California Common Core State Standards, *continued*

SE Pages	Lesson	Code	Standard
54	**Think and Respond:** Talk About It	CA CC.1.Rlit.1	Ask and answer questions about key details in a text.
		CA CC.1.Rlit.2	Retell stories, including key details, and demonstrate understanding of their central message or lesson.
			With prompting and support, read prose and poetry of appropriate complexity for grade 1.
		CA CC.1.Rlit.10.b	**Confirm predictions about what will happen next in a text. CA**
		CA CC.1.SL.6	Produce complete sentences when appropriate to task and situation. (See grade 1 Language standards 1 and 3 for specific expectations.)
		CA CC.1.W.8	With guidance and support from adults, recall information from experiences or gather information from provided sources to answer a question.
	Think and Respond: Write About It	CA CC.1.L.6	Use words and phrases acquired through conversations, reading and being read to, and responding to texts, including using frequently occurring conjunctions to signal simple relationships (e.g., *because*).
55	**Reread and Summarize:** Identify Setting	CA CC.1.Rlit.3	Describe characters, settings, and major events in a story, using key details.
		CA CC.1.W.8	With guidance and support from adults, recall information from experiences or gather information from provided sources to answer a question.
		CA CC.1.SL.1	Participate in collaborative conversations with diverse partners about *grade 1 topics and texts* with peers and adults in small and larger groups.
		CA CC.1.SL.4	Describe people, places, things, and events with relevant details, expressing ideas and feelings clearly.
		CA CC.1.SL.5	Add drawings or other visual displays to descriptions when appropriate to clarify ideas, thoughts, and feelings.
		CA CC.1.L.6	Use words and phrases acquired through conversations, reading and being read to, and responding to texts, including using frequently occurring conjunctions to signal simple relationships (e.g., *because*).
56	**Word Work:** Identify Nouns		Demonstrate command of the conventions of standard English grammar and usage when writing or speaking.
		CA CC.1.L.1.b	Use common, proper, and possessive nouns.
57-59	**Selection 2:** Postcard Greetings from Arizona	CA CC.1.Rinf.10	With prompting and support, read informational texts appropriately complex for grade 1.
		CA CC.1.Rinf.10.a	**Activate prior knowledge related to the information and events in a text. CA**

SE Pages	Lesson	Code	Standard
60	**Respond and Extend:** Compare Genres	CA CC.1.Rlit.5	Explain major differences between books that tell stories and books that give information, drawing on a wide reading of a range of text types.
		CA CC.1.Rinf.9	Identify basic similarities in and differences between two texts on the same topic (e.g., in illustrations, descriptions, or procedures).
		CA CC.1.SL.1	Participate in collaborative conversations with diverse partners about *grade 1 topics and texts* with peers and adults in small and larger groups.
		CA CC.1.SL.4	Describe people, places, things, and events with relevant details, expressing ideas and feelings clearly.
		CA CC.1.L.6	Use words and phrases acquired through conversations, reading and being read to, and responding to texts, including using frequently occurring conjunctions to signal simple relationships (e.g., *because*).
61	**Grammar and Spelling:** Proper Nouns		Demonstrate command of the conventions of standard English grammar and usage when writing or speaking.
		CA CC.1.L.1.b	Use common, proper, and possessive nouns.
			Demonstrate command of the conventions of standard English capitalization, punctuation, and spelling when writing.
		CA CC.1.L.2.a	Capitalize dates and names of people.

California Common Core State Standards, *continued*

SE Pages	Lesson	Code	Standard
62-63	**Writing Project:** Write as a Family Member	CA CC.1.W.2	Write informative/explanatory texts in which they name a topic, supply some facts about the topic, and provide some sense of closure.
		CA CC.1.W.5	With guidance and support from adults, focus on a topic, respond to questions and suggestions from peers, and add details to strengthen writing as needed.
		CA CC.1.W.6	With guidance and support from adults, use a variety of digital tools to produce and publish writing, including in collaboration with peers.
		CA CC.1.W.8	With guidance and support from adults, recall information from experiences or gather information from provided sources to answer a question.
			Participate in collaborative conversations with diverse partners about *grade 1 topics and texts* with peers and adults in small and larger groups.
		CA CC.1.SL.1.a	Follow agreed-upon rules for discussions (e.g., listening to others with care, speaking one at a time about the topics and texts under discussion).
		CA CC.1.SL.4	Describe people, places, things, and events with relevant details, expressing ideas and feelings clearly.
		CA CC.1.SL.5	Add drawings or other visual displays to descriptions when appropriate to clarify ideas, thoughts, and feelings.
			Demonstrate command of the conventions of standard English grammar and usage when writing or speaking.
		CA CC.1.L.1.b	Use common, proper, and possessive nouns.
		CA CC.1.L.1.j	Produce and expand complete simple and compound declarative, interrogative, imperative, and exclamatory sentences in response to prompts.
			Demonstrate command of the conventions of standard English capitalization, punctuation, and spelling when writing.
		CA CC.1.L.2.a	Capitalize dates and names of people.
		CA CC.1.L.2.d	Use conventional spelling for words with common spelling patterns and for frequently occurring irregular words.
		CA CC.1.L.2.e	Spell untaught words phonetically, drawing on phonemic awareness and spelling conventions.
		CA CC.1.L.6	Use words and phrases acquired through conversations, reading and being read to, and responding to texts, including using frequently occurring conjunctions to signal simple relationships (e.g., *because*).

SE Pages	Lesson	Code	Standard
64-65	**Unit Wrap-Up:** Share Your Ideas		Participate in collaborative conversations with diverse partners about *grade 1 topics and texts* with peers and adults in small and larger groups.
		CA CC.1.SL.1.a	Follow agreed-upon rules for discussions (e.g., listening to others with care, speaking one at a time about the topics and texts under discussion).
		CA CC.1.SL.1.b	Build on others' talk in conversations by responding to the comments of others through multiple exchanges.
		CA CC.1.SL.4	Describe people, places, things, and events with relevant details, expressing ideas and feelings clearly.
		CA CC.1.SL.5	Add drawings or other visual displays to descriptions when appropriate to clarify ideas, thoughts, and feelings.
		CA CC.1.L.6	Use words and phrases acquired through conversations, reading and being read to, and responding to texts, including using frequently occurring conjunctions to signal simple relationships (e.g., *because*).

SE Pages	Lesson	Code	Standard
66–67	**Unit Launch:** Share What You Know		With prompting and support, read prose and poetry of appropriate complexity for grade 1.
		CA CC.1.Rlit.10.a	**Activate prior knowledge related to the information and events in a text. CA**
		CA CC.1.SL.4	Describe people, places, things, and events with relevant details, expressing ideas and feelings clearly.
68	**Part 1: Language:** Describe	CA CC.1.SL.4	Describe people, places, things, and events with relevant details, expressing ideas and feelings clearly.
		CA CC.1.SL.4.a	**Memorize and recite poems, rhymes, and songs with expression. CA**
69	**Science Vocabulary:** Key Words		With guidance and support from adults, demonstrate understanding of word relationships and nuances in word meanings.
		CA CC.1.L.5.b	Define words by category and by one or more key attributes (e.g., a *duck* is a bird that swims; *tiger* is a large cat with stripes).
70	**Thinking Map:** List Facts		With prompting and support, read informational texts appropriately complex for grade 1.
		CA CC.1.Rinf.10.a	**Activate prior knowledge related to the information and events in a text. CA**
		CA CC.1.SL.4	Describe people, places, things, and events with relevant details, expressing ideas and feelings clearly.

California Common Core State Standards, *continued*

SE Pages	Lesson	Code	Standard
71	**Academic Vocabulary:** More Key Words		Determine or clarify the meaning of unknown and multiple-meaning words and phrases based on *grade 1 reading and content,* choosing flexibly from an array of strategies.
		CA CC.1.L.4.a	Use sentence-level context as a clue to the meaning of a word or phrase.
72	**Selection 1 Preview:** Read a Song		Read with sufficient accuracy and fluency to support comprehension.
		CA CC.1.Rfou.4.a	Read on-level text with purpose and understanding.
73–85	**Selection 1: Song** Are You Living?	CA CC.1.Rlit.10	With prompting and support, read prose and poetry of appropriate complexity for grade 1.
86	**Think and Respond:** Talk About It	CA CC.1.Rinf.1	Ask and answer questions about key details in a text.
			Read with sufficient accuracy and fluency to support comprehension.
		CA CC.1.Rfou.4.a	Read on-level text with purpose and understanding.
		CA CC.1.SL.6	Produce complete sentences when appropriate to task and situation. (See grade 1 Language standards 1 and 3 for specific expectations.)
		CA CC.1.L.6	Use words and phrases acquired through conversations, reading and being read to, and responding to texts, including using frequently occurring conjunctions to signal simple relationships (e.g., *because*).
	Think and Respond: Write About It	CA CC.1.W.8	With guidance and support from adults, recall information from experiences or gather information from provided sources to answer a question.
		CA CC.1.L.6	Use words and phrases acquired through conversations, reading and being read to, and responding to texts, including using frequently occurring conjunctions to signal simple relationships (e.g., *because*).
87	**Reread and Describe:** List Facts	CA CC.1.Rinf.2	Identify the main topic and retell key details of a text.
		CA CC.1.Rinf.7	Use the illustrations and details in a text to describe its key ideas.
		CA CC.1.W.8	With guidance and support from adults, recall information from experiences or gather information from provided sources to answer a question.
		CA CC.1.SL.1	Participate in collaborative conversations with diverse partners about *grade 1 topics and texts* with peers and adults in small and larger groups.
88	**Word Work:** Sort Words		With guidance and support from adults, demonstrate understanding of word relationships and nuances in word meanings.
		CA CC.1.L.5.a	Sort words into categories (e.g., colors, clothing) to gain a sense of the concepts the categories represent.
		CA CC.1.L.5.b	Define words by category and by one or more key attributes (e.g., a *duck* is a bird that swims; *tiger* is a large cat with stripes).

SE Pages	Lesson	Code	Standard
89–91	**Selection 2: Diagram** A Straw Hat	CA CC.1.Rinf.10	With prompting and support, read informational texts appropriately complex for grade 1.
92	**Respond and Extend:** Compare Genres	CA CC.1.Rinf.2	Identify the main topic and retell key details of a text.
		CA CC.1.Rinf.9	Identify basic similarities in and differences between two texts on the same topic (e.g., in illustrations, descriptions, or procedures).
		CA CC.1.SL.1	Participate in collaborative conversations with diverse partners about *grade 1 topics and texts* with peers and adults in small and larger groups.
		CA CC.1.L.6	Use words and phrases acquired through conversations, reading and being read to, and responding to texts, including using frequently occurring conjunctions to signal simple relationships (e.g., *because*).
93	**Grammar: Adjectives**		Demonstrate command of the conventions of standard English grammar and usage when writing or speaking.
		CA CC.1.L.1.f	Use frequently occurring adjectives.
94	**Part 2:** **Language:** Retell a Story	CA CC.1.SL.4	Describe people, places, things, and events with relevant details, expressing ideas and feelings clearly.
		CA CC.1.SL.4.a	**Memorize and recite poems, rhymes, and songs with expression. CA**
95	**Science Vocabulary:** Key Words	CA CC.1.SL.1	Participate in collaborative conversations with diverse partners about *grade 1 topics and texts* with peers and adults in small and larger groups.
			Determine or clarify the meaning of unknown and multiple-meaning words and phrases based on *grade 1 reading and content,* choosing flexibly from an array of strategies.
		CA CC.1.L.5.c	Identify real-life connections between words and their use (e.g., note places at home that are *cozy*).
96	**Thinking Map:** Identify Plot	CA CC.1.Rlit.2	Retell stories, including key details, and demonstrate understanding of their central message or lesson.
			Participate in collaborative conversations with diverse partners about *grade 1 topics and texts* with peers and adults in small and larger groups.
		CA CC.1.SL.1.a	Follow agreed-upon rules for discussions (e.g., listening to others with care, speaking one at a time about the topics and texts under discussion).
97	**Academic Vocabulary:** More Key Words		Determine or clarify the meaning of unknown and multiple-meaning words and phrases based on *grade 1 reading and content*, choosing flexibly from an array of strategies.
		CA CC.1.L.4.a	Use sentence-level context as a clue to the meaning of a word or phrase.
98	**Selection 1 Preview:** Read a Folk Tale		Read with sufficient accuracy and fluency to support comprehension.
		CA CC.1.Rfou.4.a	Read on-level text with purpose and understanding.

California Common Core State Standards, *continued*

SE Pages	Lesson	Code	Standard
99–116	**Selection 1:** Folk Tale The Daisy	CA CC.1.Rlit.10	With prompting and support, read prose and poetry of appropriate complexity for grade 1.
117	**Meet the Author:** Writer's Craft	CA CC.1.Rlit.7	Use illustrations and details in a story to describe its characters, setting, or events.
118	**Think and Respond:** Talk About It	CA CC.1.Rlit.1	Ask and answer questions about key details in a text.
		CA CC.1.SL.6	Produce complete sentences when appropriate to task and situation. (See grade 1 Language standards 1 and 3 for specific expectations.)
		CA CC.1.L.6	Use words and phrases acquired through conversations, reading and being read to, and responding to texts, including using frequently occurring conjunctions to signal simple relationships (e.g., *because*).
	Think and Respond: Write About It	CA CC.1.W.8	With guidance and support from adults, recall information from experiences or gather information from provided sources to answer a question.
		CA CC.1.L.6	Use words and phrases acquired through conversations, reading and being read to, and responding to texts, including using frequently occurring conjunctions to signal simple relationships (e.g., *because*).
119	**Reread and Describe:** Identify Plot	CA CC.1.Rlit.3	Describe characters, settings, and major events in a story, using key details.
		CA CC.1.W.8	With guidance and support from adults, recall information from experiences or gather information from provided sources to answer a question.
		CA CC.1.SL.1	Participate in collaborative conversations with diverse partners about *grade 1 topics and texts* with peers and adults in small and larger groups.
		CA CC.1.SL.4	Describe people, places, things, and events with relevant details, expressing ideas and feelings clearly.
		CA CC.1.L.6	Use words and phrases acquired through conversations, reading and being read to, and responding to texts, including using frequently occurring conjunctions to signal simple relationships (e.g., *because*).
120	**Word Work:** Sort Words		With guidance and support from adults, demonstrate understanding of word relationships and nuances in word meanings.
		CA CC.1.L.5.a	Sort words into categories (e.g., colors, clothing) to gain a sense of the concepts the categories represent.
		CA CC.1.L.5.b	Define words by category and by one or more key attributes (e.g., a *duck* is a bird that swims; a *tiger* is a large cat with stripes).
121–125	**Selection 2:** Project Notebook Michael Fay and the Giant Redwoods	CA CC.1.Rinf.10	With prompting and support, read informational texts appropriately complex for grade 1.
		CA CC.1.Rinf.10.a	**Activate prior knowledge related to the information and events in a text. CA**

SE Pages	Lesson	Code	Standard
126	**Respond and Extend:** Compare Genres	CA CC.1.Rlit.5	Explain major differences between books that tell stories and books that give information, drawing on a wide reading of a range of text types.
		CA CC.1.Rinf.9	Identify basic similarities in and differences between two texts on the same topic (e.g., in illustrations, descriptions, or procedures).
		CA CC.1.SL.1	Participate in collaborative conversations with diverse partners about *grade 1 topics and texts* with peers and adults in small and larger groups.
		CA CC.1.SL.4	Describe people, places, things, and events with relevant details, expressing ideas and feelings clearly.
		CA CC.1.L.6	Use words and phrases acquired through conversations, reading and being read to, and responding to texts, including using frequently occurring conjunctions to signal simple relationships (e.g., *because*).
127	**Grammar:** Adjectives		Demonstrate command of the conventions of standard English grammar and usage when writing or speaking.
		CA CC.1.L.1.f	Use frequently occurring adjectives.
128–129	**Writing Project:** Write Like a Teacher	CA CC.1.W.2	Write informative/explanatory texts in which they name a topic, supply some facts about the topic, and provide some sense of closure.
		CA CC.1.W.5	With guidance and support from adults, focus on a topic, respond to questions and suggestions from peers, and add details to strengthen writing as needed.
		CA CC.1.W.8	With guidance and support from adults, recall information from experiences or gather information from provided sources to answer a question.
			Participate in collaborative conversations with diverse partners about *grade 1 topics and texts* with peers and adults in small and larger groups.
		CA CC.1.SL.1.a	Follow agreed-upon rules for discussions (e.g., listening to others with care, speaking one at a time about the topics and texts under discussion).
		CA CC.1.SL.4	Describe people, places, things, and events with relevant details, expressing ideas and feelings clearly.
		CA CC.1.SL.5	Add drawings or other visual displays to descriptions when appropriate to clarify ideas, thoughts, and feelings.
			Demonstrate command of the conventions of standard English grammar and usage when writing or speaking.
		CA CC.1.L.1.f	Use frequently occurring adjectives.
			Demonstrate command of the conventions of standard English capitalization, punctuation, and spelling when writing.
		CA CC.1.L.2.d	Use conventional spelling for words with common spelling patterns and for frequently occurring irregular words.
		CA CC.1.L.2.e	Spell untaught words phonetically, drawing on phonemic awareness and spelling conventions.
		CA CC.1.L.6	Use words and phrases acquired through conversations, reading and being read to, and responding to texts, including using frequently occurring conjunctions to signal simple relationships (e.g., *because*).

California Common Core State Standards, *continued*

SE Pages	Lesson	Code	Standard
130–131	**Unit Wrap-Up:** **Share Your Ideas**	CA CC.1.W.8	With guidance and support from adults, recall information from experiences or gather information from provided sources to answer a question.
			Participate in collaborative conversations with diverse partners about *grade 1 topics and texts* with peers and adults in small and larger groups.
		CA CC.1.SL.1.a	Follow agreed-upon rules for discussions (e.g., listening to others with care, speaking one at a time about the topics and texts under discussion).
		CA CC.1.SL.1.b	Build on others' talk in conversations by responding to the comments of others through multiple exchanges.
		CA CC.1.SL.4	Describe people, places, things, and events with relevant details, expressing ideas and feelings clearly.
		CA CC.1.SL.5	Add drawings or other visual displays to descriptions when appropriate to clarify ideas, thoughts, and feelings.
			With guidance and support from adults, demonstrate understanding of word relationships and nuances in word meanings.
		CA CC.1.L.5.a	Sort words into categories (e.g., colors, clothing) to gain a sense of the concepts the categories represent.
		CA CC.1.L.6	Use words and phrases acquired through conversations, reading and being read to, and responding to texts, including using frequently occurring conjunctions to signal simple relationships (e.g., *because*).

SE Pages	Lesson	Code	Standard
132–133	**Unit Launch:** Share What You Know		With prompting and support, read prose and poetry of appropriate complexity for grade 1.
		CA CC.1.Rlit.10.a	**Activate prior knowledge related to the information and events in a text. CA**
		CA CC.1.SL.4	Describe people, places, things, and events with relevant details, expressing ideas and feelings clearly.
		CA CC.1.SL.5	Add drawings or other visual displays to descriptions when appropriate to clarify ideas, thoughts, and feelings.
134	**Part 1: Language:** Express Needs and Wants	CA CC.1.SL.4	Describe people, places, things, and events with relevant details, expressing ideas and feelings clearly.
		CA CC.1.SL.4.a	**Memorize and recite poems, rhymes, and songs with expression. CA**
135	**Social Studies** **Vocabulary:** Key Words		Determine or clarify the meaning of unknown and multiple-meaning words and phrases based on *grade 1 reading and content,* choosing flexibly from an array of strategies.
		CA CC.1.L.4.a	Use sentence-level context as a clue to the meaning of a word or phrase.

SE Pages	Lesson	Code	Standard
136	**Thinking Map:** Categorize		With guidance and support from adults, demonstrate understanding of word relationships and nuances in word meanings.
		CA CC.1.L.5.a	Sort words into categories (e.g., colors, clothing) to gain a sense of the concepts the categories represent.
137	**Academic Vocabulary:** More Key Words		Determine or clarify the meaning of unknown and multiple-meaning words and phrases based on *grade 1 reading and content,* choosing flexibly from an array of strategies.
		CA CC.1.L.4.a	Use sentence-level context as a clue to the meaning of a word or phrase.
		CA CC.1.L.6	Use words and phrases acquired through conversations, reading and being read to, and responding to texts, including using frequently occurring conjunctions to signal simple relationships (e.g., *because*).
138	**Selection 1 Preview:** Read a Social Studies Article	CA CC.1.Rinf.5	Know and use various text **structures (e.g., sequence) and text** features (e.g., headings, tables of contents, glossaries, electronic menus, icons) to locate key facts or information in a text. **CA**
			Read with sufficient accuracy and fluency to support comprehension.
		CA CC.1.Rfou.4.a	Read on-level text with purpose and understanding.
139–153	**Selection 1:** Social Studies Article Markets	CA CC.1.Rinf.10	With prompting and support, read informational texts appropriately complex for grade 1.
154	**Think and Respond:** Talk About It	CA CC.1.Rinf.1	Ask and answer questions about key details in a text.
		CA CC.1.Rinf.2	Identify the main topic and retell key details of a text.
		CA CC.1.Rinf.7	Use the illustrations and details in a text to describe its key ideas.
		CA CC.1.SL.6	Produce complete sentences when appropriate to task and situation. (See grade 1 Language standards 1 and 3 for specific expectations.)
	Think and Respond: Write About It	CA CC.1.L.6	Use words and phrases acquired through conversations, reading and being read to, and responding to texts, including using frequently occurring conjunctions to signal simple relationships (e.g., *because*).

California Common Core State Standards, *continued*

SE Pages	Lesson	Code	Standard
155	**Reread and Retell:** Categorize	CA CC.1.Rinf.1	Ask and answer questions about key details in a text.
		CA CC.1.W.8	With guidance and support from adults, recall information from experiences or gather information from provided sources to answer a question.
		CA CC.1.SL.1	Participate in collaborative conversations with diverse partners about *grade 1 topics and texts* with peers and adults in small and larger groups.
			With guidance and support from adults, demonstrate understanding of word relationships and nuances in word meanings.
		CA CC.1.L.5.a	Sort words into categories (e.g., colors, clothing) to gain a sense of the concepts the categories represent.
		CA CC.1.L.5.b	Define words by category and by one or more key attributes (e.g., a *duck* is a bird that swims; a *tiger* is a large cat with stripes).
156	**Word Work:** Identify Verbs	CA CC.1.L.1	Demonstrate command of the conventions of standard English grammar and usage when writing or speaking.
157–159	**Selection 2:** Online Article Flower Power	CA CC.1.Rinf.10	With prompting and support, read informational texts appropriately complex for grade 1.
160	**Respond and Extend:** Compare Author's Purpose	CA CC.1.Rinf.2	Identify the main topic and retell key details of a text.
		CA CC.1.Rinf.9	Identify basic similarities in and differences between two texts on the same topic (e.g., in illustrations, descriptions, or procedures).
		CA CC.1.SL.1	Participate in collaborative conversations with diverse partners about *grade 1 topics and texts* with peers and adults in small and larger groups.
		CA CC.1.L.6	Use words and phrases acquired through conversations, reading and being read to, and responding to texts, including using frequently occurring conjunctions to signal simple relationships (e.g., *because*).
161	**Grammar:** Present Tense Verbs		Know and apply grade-level phonics and word analysis skills in decoding words **both in isolation and in text. CA**
		CA CC.1.Rfou.3.f	Read words with inflectional endings.
			Demonstrate command of the conventions of standard English grammar and usage when writing or speaking.
		CA CC.1.L.1.e	Use verbs to convey a sense of past, present, and future (e.g., *Yesterday I walked home; Today I walk home; Tomorrow I will walk home*).
			Determine or clarify the meaning of unknown and multiple-meaning words and phrases based on *grade 1 reading and content,* choosing flexibly from an array of strategies.
		CA CC.1.L.4.c	Identify frequently occurring root words (e.g., *look*) and their inflectional forms (e.g., *looks, looked, looking*).

SE Pages	Lesson	Code	Standard
162	**Part 2:** **Language:** Ask Questions		Participate in collaborative conversations with diverse partners about *grade 1 topics and texts* with peers and adults in small and larger groups.
		CA CC.1.SL.1.c	Ask questions to clear up any confusion about the topics and texts under discussion.
			Describe people, places, things, and events with relevant details, expressing ideas and feelings clearly.
		CA CC.1.SL.4.a	**Memorize and recite poems, rhymes, and songs with expression. CA**
163	**Social Studies** **Vocabulary:** Key Words		Participate in collaborative conversations with diverse partners about *grade 1 topics and texts* with peers and adults in small and larger groups.
		CA CC.1.SL.1.c	Ask questions to clear up any confusion about the topics and texts under discussion.
		CA CC.1.SL.2	Ask and answer questions about key details in a text read aloud or information presented orally or through other media.
		CA CC.1.SL.2.a	**Give, restate, and follow simple two-step directions. CA**
			Determine or clarify the meaning of unknown and multiple-meaning words and phrases based on *grade 1 reading and content,* choosing flexibly from an array of strategies.
		CA CC.1.L.4.a	Use sentence-level context as a clue to the meaning of a word or phrase.
164	**Thinking Map:** Identify Details	CA CC.1.W.8	With guidance and support from adults, recall information from experiences or gather information from provided sources to answer a question.
		CA CC.1.SL.4	Describe people, places, things, and events with relevant details, expressing ideas and feelings clearly.
		CA CC.1.SL.5	Add drawings or other visual displays to descriptions when appropriate to clarify ideas, thoughts, and feelings.
165	**Academic Vocabulary:** More Key Words		Determine or clarify the meaning of unknown and multiple-meaning words and phrases based on *grade 1 reading and content,* choosing flexibly from an array of strategies.
		CA CC.1.L.4.a	Use sentence-level context as a clue to the meaning of a word or phrase.
166	**Selection 1 Preview:** Read a Poem		Read with sufficient accuracy and fluency to support comprehension.
		CA CC.1.Rfou.4.a	Read on-level text with purpose and understanding.
167–185	**Selection 1: Poem** Delivery	CA CC.1.Rlit.10	With prompting and support, read prose and poetry of appropriate complexity for grade 1.
186	**Meet the Author:** Writer's Craft	CA CC.1.Rlit.7	Use illustrations and details in a story to describe its characters, setting, or events.
		CA CC.1.W.8	With guidance and support from adults, recall information from experiences or gather information from provided sources to answer a question.
		CA CC.1.L.5	With guidance and support from adults, demonstrate understanding of word relationships and nuances in word meanings.

California Common Core State Standards, *continued*

SE Pages	Lesson	Code	Standard
188	**Think and Respond:** Talk About It	CA CC.1.Rlit.1	Ask and answer questions about key details in a text.
		CA CC.1.SL.6	Produce complete sentences when appropriate to task and situation. (See grade 1 Language standards 1 and 3 for specific expectations.)
		CA CC.1.L.6	Use words and phrases acquired through conversations, reading and being read to, and responding to texts, including using frequently occurring conjunctions to signal simple relationships (e.g., *because*).
	Think and Respond: Write About It	CA CC.1.L.6	Use words and phrases acquired through conversations, reading and being read to, and responding to texts, including using frequently occurring conjunctions to signal simple relationships (e.g., *because*).
189	**Reread and Retell:** Identify Details	CA CC.1.Rlit.2	Retell stories, including key details, and demonstrate understanding of their central message or lesson.
		CA CC.1.Rlit.2	Retell stories, including key details, and demonstrate understanding of their central message or lesson.
		CA CC.1.L.6	Use words and phrases acquired through conversations, reading and being read to, and responding to texts, including using frequently occurring conjunctions to signal simple relationships (e.g., *because*).
190	**Word Work:** Identify Verbs	CA CC.1.L.1	Demonstrate command of the conventions of standard English grammar and usage when writing or speaking.
191–193	**Selection 2:** Fact Sheet Money	CA CC.1.Rinf.10	With prompting and support, read informational texts appropriately complex for grade 1.
		CA CC.1.Rinf.10.a	**Activate prior knowledge related to the information and events in a text. CA**
194	**Respond and Extend:** Compare Genres	CA CC.1.Rlit.5	Explain major differences between books that tell stories and books that give information, drawing on a wide reading of a range of text types.
		CA CC.1.SL.1	Participate in collaborative conversations with diverse partners about *grade 1 topics and texts* with peers and adults in small and larger groups.
		CA CC.1.L.6	Use words and phrases acquired through conversations, reading and being read to, and responding to texts, including using frequently occurring conjunctions to signal simple relationships (e.g., *because*).
195	**Grammar and Spelling:** Subject-Verb Agreement: *be* and *have*		Demonstrate command of the conventions of standard English grammar and usage when writing or speaking.
		CA CC.1.L.1.c	Use singular and plural nouns with matching verbs in basic sentences (e.g., *He hops; We hop*).

SE Pages	Lesson	Code	Standard
196–197	**Writing Project:** Write as a Family Member	CA CC.1.W.1	Write opinion pieces in which they introduce the topic or name the book they are writing about, state an opinion, supply a reason for the opinion, and provide some sense of closure.
		CA CC.1.W.5	With guidance and support from adults, focus on a topic, respond to questions and suggestions from peers, and add details to strengthen writing as needed.
		CA CC.1.W.8	With guidance and support from adults, recall information from experiences or gather information from provided sources to answer a question.
		CA CC.1.SL.4	Describe people, places, things, and events with relevant details, expressing ideas and feelings clearly.
			Demonstrate command of the conventions of standard English grammar and usage when writing or speaking.
		CA CC.1.L.1.c	Use singular and plural nouns with matching verbs in basic sentences (e.g., *He hops; We hop*).
			Demonstrate command of the conventions of standard English capitalization, punctuation, and spelling when writing.
		CA CC.1.L.2.d	Use conventional spelling for words with common spelling patterns and for frequently occurring irregular words.
		CA CC.1.L.2.e	Spell untaught words phonetically, drawing on phonemic awareness and spelling conventions.
198–199	**Unit Wrap-Up:** Share Your Ideas		Participate in collaborative conversations with diverse partners about *grade 1 topics and texts* with peers and adults in small and larger groups.
		CA CC.1.SL.1.a	Follow agreed-upon rules for discussions (e.g., listening to others with care, speaking one at a time about the topics and texts under discussion).
		CA CC.1.SL.1.b	Build on others' talk in conversations by responding to the comments of others through multiple exchanges.
		CA CC.1.SL.4	Describe people, places, things, and events with relevant details, expressing ideas and feelings clearly.
			With guidance and support from adults, demonstrate understanding of word relationships and nuances in word meanings.
		CA CC.1.L.5.a	Sort words into categories (e.g., colors, clothing) to gain a sense of the concepts the categories represent.
		CA CC.1.L.5.b	Define words by category and by one or more key attributes (e.g., a *duck* is a bird that swims; a *tiger* is a large cat with stripes).
		CA CC.1.L.6	Use words and phrases acquired through conversations, reading and being read to, and responding to texts, including using frequently occurring conjunctions to signal simple relationships (e.g., *because*).

California Common Core State Standards, *continued*

SE Pages	Lesson	Code	Standard
200–201	**Unit Launch:** Share What You Know		With prompting and support, read informational texts appropriately complex for grade 1.
		CA CC.1.Rinf.10.a	**Activate prior knowledge related to the information and events in a text. CA**
		CA CC.1.SL.4	Describe people, places, things, and events with relevant details, expressing ideas and feelings clearly.
		CA CC.1.SL.5	Add drawings or other visual displays to descriptions when appropriate to clarify ideas, thoughts, and feelings.
202	**Part 1:** **Language:** Retell a Story	CA CC.1.SL.4	Describe people, places, things, and events with relevant details, expressing ideas and feelings clearly.
		CA CC.1.SL.4.a	**Memorize and recite poems, rhymes, and songs with expression. CA**
203	**Science Vocabulary:** Key Words	CA CC.1.SL.4	Describe people, places, things, and events with relevant details, expressing ideas and feelings clearly.
			Determine or clarify the meaning of unknown and multiple-meaning words and phrases based on *grade 1 reading and content,* choosing flexibly from an array of strategies.
		CA CC.1.L.4.a	Use sentence-level context as a clue to the meaning of a word or phrase.
204	**Thinking Map:** Identify Plot	CA CC.1.Rlit.2	Retell stories, including key details, and demonstrate understanding of their central message or lesson.
		CA CC.1.SL.4	Describe people, places, things, and events with relevant details, expressing ideas and feelings clearly.
205	**Academic Vocabulary:** More Key Words		Determine or clarify the meaning of unknown and multiple-meaning words and phrases based on *grade 1 reading and content,* choosing flexibly from an array of strategies.
		CA CC.1.L.4.a	Use sentence-level context as a clue to the meaning of a word or phrase.
		CA CC.1.L.6	Use words and phrases acquired through conversations, reading and being read to, and responding to texts, including using frequently occurring conjunctions to signal simple relationships (e.g., *because*).
206	**Selection 1 Preview:** Read a Story	CA CC.1.Rlit.7	Use illustrations and details in a story to describe its characters, setting, or events.
			Read with sufficient accuracy and fluency to support comprehension.
		CA CC.1.Rfou.4.a	Read on-level text with purpose and understanding.
207–230	**Selection 1: Story** Ruby in Her Own Time	CA CC.1.Rlit.10	With prompting and support, read prose and poetry of appropriate complexity for grade 1.
231	**Meet the Author:** Writer's Craft	CA CC.1.Rlit.4	Identify words and phrases in stories or poems that suggest feelings or appeal to the senses. **(See grade 1 Language standards 4–6 for additional expectations.) CA**

SE Pages	Lesson	Code	Standard
232	**Think and Respond:** Talk About It	CA CC.1.Rlit.1	Ask and answer questions about key details in a text.
		CA CC.1.Rlit.2	Retell stories, including key details, and demonstrate understanding of their central message or lesson.
		CA CC.1.Rlit.7	Use illustrations and details in a story to describe its characters, setting, or events.
		CA CC.1.SL.6	Produce complete sentences when appropriate to task and situation. (See grade 1 Language standards 1 and 3 for specific expectations.)
		CA CC.1.L.6	Use words and phrases acquired through conversations, reading and being read to, and responding to texts, including using frequently occurring conjunctions to signal simple relationships (e.g., *because*).
	Think and Respond: Write About It	CA CC.1.Rlit.3	Describe characters, settings, and major events in a story, using key details.
		CA CC.1.W.8	With guidance and support from adults, recall information from experiences or gather information from provided sources to answer a question.
233	**Reread and Retell:** Identify Plot	CA CC.1.Rlit.2	Retell stories, including key details, and demonstrate understanding of their central message or lesson.
		CA CC.1.Rlit.3	Describe characters, settings, and major events in a story, using key details.
234	**Word Work:** Use Context Clues		Determine or clarify the meaning of unknown and multiple-meaning words and phrases based on *grade 1 reading and content*, choosing flexibly from an array of strategies.
		CA CC.1.L.4.a	Use sentence-level context as a clue to the meaning of a word or phrase.
235–239	**Selection 2:** Science Article Turtles: From Eggs to Ocean	CA CC.1.Rinf.10	With prompting and support, read informational texts appropriately complex for grade 1.
240	**Respond and Extend:** Compare Genres	CA CC.1.Rlit.5	Explain major differences between books that tell stories and books that give information, drawing on a wide reading of a range of text types.
		CA CC.1.Rinf.9	Identify basic similarities in and differences between two texts on the same topic (e.g., in illustrations, descriptions, or procedures).
		CA CC.1.SL.4	Describe people, places, things, and events with relevant details, expressing ideas and feelings clearly.
241	**Grammar:** Subject Pronouns		Demonstrate command of the conventions of standard English grammar and usage when writing or speaking.
		CA CC.1.L.1.d	Use personal **(subject, object)**, possessive, and indefinite pronouns (e.g., *I, me, my; they, them, their; anyone, everything*). *CA*

California Common Core State Standards, *continued*

SE Pages	Lesson	Code	Standard
242	**Part 2:** **Language:** Restate an Idea	CA CC.1.SL.4	Describe people, places, things, and events with relevant details, expressing ideas and feelings clearly.
		CA CC.1.SL.4.a	**Memorize and recite poems, rhymes, and songs with expression. CA**
243	**Science Vocabulary:** Key Words	CA CC.1.SL.1	Participate in collaborative conversations with diverse partners about *grade 1 topics and texts* with peers and adults in small and larger groups.
			Determine or clarify the meaning of unknown and multiple-meaning words and phrases based on *grade 1 reading and content,* choosing flexibly from an array of strategies.
		CA CC.1.L.4.a	Use sentence-level context as a clue to the meaning of a word or phrase.
		CA CC.1.L.6	Use words and phrases acquired through conversations, reading and being read to, and responding to texts, including using frequently occurring conjunctions to signal simple relationships (e.g., *because*).
244	**Thinking Map:** Identify Main Idea and Details	CA CC.1.Rinf.2	Identify the main topic and retell key details of a text.
		CA CC.1.SL.4	Describe people, places, things, and events with relevant details, expressing ideas and feelings clearly.
		CA CC.1.L.6	Use words and phrases acquired through conversations, reading and being read to, and responding to texts, including using frequently occurring conjunctions to signal simple relationships (e.g., *because*).
245	**Academic Vocabulary:** **More Key Words**		Determine or clarify the meaning of unknown and multiple-meaning words and phrases based on *grade 1 reading and content,* choosing flexibly from an array of strategies.
		CA CC.1.L.4.a	Use sentence-level context as a clue to the meaning of a word or phrase.
246	**Selection 1 Preview:** Read a Science Article	CA CC.1.Rinf.5	Know and use various text **structures (e.g., sequence) and text** features (e.g., headings, tables of contents, glossaries, electronic menus, icons) to locate key facts or information in a text. CA
			Read with sufficient accuracy and fluency to support comprehension.
		CA CC.1.Rfou.4.a	Read on-level text with purpose and understanding.
247–257	**Selection 1:** Science Article A Butterfly Is Born	CA CC.1.Rinf.10	With prompting and support, read informational texts appropriately complex for grade 1.
258	**Think and Respond:** Talk About It	CA CC.1.Rinf.1	Ask and answer questions about key details in a text.
		CA CC.1.Rinf.3	Describe the connection between two individuals, events, ideas, or pieces of information in a text.
		CA CC.1.Rinf.7	Use the illustrations and details in a text to describe its key ideas.
		CA CC.1.SL.6	Produce complete sentences when appropriate to task and situation. (See grade 1 Language standards 1 and 3 for specific expectations.)

Unit 4 Growing and Changing, continued

SE Pages	Lesson	Code	Standard
	Think and Respond: Write About It	CA CC.1.W.8	With guidance and support from adults, recall information from experiences or gather information from provided sources to answer a question.
		CA CC.1.L.6	Use words and phrases acquired through conversations, reading and being read to, and responding to texts, including using frequently occurring conjunctions to signal simple relationships (e.g., *because*).
259	**Reread and Summarize:** Identify Main Idea and Details	CA CC.1.Rinf.2	Identify the main topic and retell key details of a text.
		CA CC.1.W.8	With guidance and support from adults, recall information from experiences or gather information from provided sources to answer a question.
		CA CC.1.SL.4	Describe people, places, things, and events with relevant details, expressing ideas and feelings clearly.
		CA CC.1.L.6	Use words and phrases acquired through conversations, reading and being read to, and responding to texts, including using frequently occurring conjunctions to signal simple relationships (e.g., *because*).
260	**Word Work:** Use Context Clues		Determine or clarify the meaning of unknown and multiple-meaning words and phrases based on *grade 1 reading and content,* choosing flexibly from an array of strategies.
		CA CC.1.L.4.a	Use sentence-level context as a clue to the meaning of a word or phrase.
261–263	**Selection 2:** Poem Caterpillar	CA CC.1.Rlit.10	With prompting and support, read prose and poetry of appropriate complexity for grade 1.
264	**Respond and Extend:** Compare Genres	CA CC.1.Rlit.5	Explain major differences between books that tell stories and books that give information, drawing on a wide reading of a range of text types.
		CA CC.1.Rinf.9	Identify basic similarities in and differences between two texts on the same topic (e.g., in illustrations, descriptions, or procedures).
		CA CC.1.SL.1	Participate in collaborative conversations with diverse partners about *grade 1 topics and texts* with peers and adults in small and larger groups.
		CA CC.1.SL.4	Describe people, places, things, and events with relevant details, expressing ideas and feelings clearly.
		CA CC.1.L.6	Use words and phrases acquired through conversations, reading and being read to, and responding to texts, including using frequently occurring conjunctions to signal simple relationships (e.g., *because*).
265	**Grammar:** Possessive Words		Demonstrate command of the conventions of standard English grammar and usage when writing or speaking.
		CA CC.1.L.1.b	Use common, proper, and possessive nouns.
		CA CC.1.L.1.d	Use personal **(subject, object)**, possessive, and indefinite pronouns (e.g., *I, me, my; they, them, their; anyone, everything*). CA

California Common Core State Standards, *continued*

SE Pages	Lesson	Code	Standard
266–267	**Writing Project:** Write Like a Storyteller	CA CC.1.W.3	Write narratives in which they recount two or more appropriately sequenced events, in- clude some details regarding what happened, use temporal words to signal event order, and provide some sense of closure.
		CA CC.1.W.5	With guidance and support from adults, focus on a topic, respond to questions and suggestions from peers, and add details to strengthen writing as needed.
			Participate in collaborative conversations with diverse partners about *grade 1 topics and texts* with peers and adults in small and larger groups.
		CA CC.1.SL.1.a	Follow agreed-upon rules for discussions (e.g., listening to others with care, speaking one at a time about the topics and texts under discussion).
		CA CC.1.SL.4	Describe people, places, things, and events with relevant details, expressing ideas and feelings clearly.
			Demonstrate command of the conventions of standard English grammar and usage when writing or speaking.
		CA CC.1.L.1.d	Use personal **(subject, object)**, possessive, and indefinite pronouns (e.g., *I, me, my; they, them, their; anyone, everything*). CA
			Demonstrate command of the conventions of standard English capitalization, punctuation, and spelling when writing.
		CA CC.1.L.2.d	Use conventional spelling for words with common spelling patterns and for frequently occurring irregular words.
		CA CC.1.L.2.e	Spell untaught words phonetically, drawing on phonemic awareness and spelling conventions.
268–269	**Unit Wrap-Up:** Share Your Ideas	CA CC.1.W.8	With guidance and support from adults, recall information from experiences or gather information from provided sources to answer a question.
			Participate in collaborative conversations with diverse partners about *grade 1 topics and texts* with peers and adults in small and larger groups.
		CA CC.1.SL.1.c	Ask questions to clear up any confusion about the topics and texts under discussion.
		CA CC.1.SL.2	Ask and answer questions about key details in a text read aloud or information presented orally or through other media.
		CA CC.1.SL.4	Describe people, places, things, and events with relevant details, expressing ideas and feelings clearly.
		CA CC.1.SL.5	Add drawings or other visual displays to descriptions when appropriate to clarify ideas, thoughts, and feelings.
		CA CC.1.L.6	Use words and phrases acquired through conversations, reading and being read to, and responding to texts, including using frequently occurring conjunctions to signal simple relationships (e.g., *because*).